QUICK AND EASY
GRAMMAR GAMES TO
BOOST WRITING POWER

QUICK AND EASY GRAMMAR GAMES TO BOOST WRITING POWER

Catherine DePino, Ed.D.

Teacher Ideas Press, an imprint of Libraries Unlimited

Westport, Connecticut · London

Library of Congress Cataloging-in-Publication Data

DePino, Catherine.
  Quick and easy grammar games to boost writing power / by Catherine DePino.
    p.   cm.
  Includes bibliographical references and index.
  ISBN 1-59158-328-4 (pbk. : alk. paper)
  1. English language—Composition and exercises—Study and teaching
(Elementary)—Activity programs. I. Title.
LB1576.D437   2006
  372.62'3--dc22   2005030819

British Library Cataloguing in Publication Data is available.

Library of Congress Catalog Card Number: 2005030819
ISBN: 1-59158-328-4

First published in 2006

Libraries Unlimited/Teacher Ideas Press, 88 Post Road West, Westport, CT 06881
A Member of the Greenwood Publishing Group, Inc.
www.lu.com

Printed in the United States of America

The paper used in this book complies with the
Permanent Paper Standard issued by the National
Information Standards Organization (Z39.48–1984).

10   9   8   7   6   5   4   3   2   1

To my daughter, Lauren Marie, singer and wordsmith:
"Sing again, with your dear voice revealing
A tone of some world far from ours . . ."
Percy Bysshe Shelley

CONTENTS

ACKNOWLEDGMENTS

Thanks to Sharon Coatney, acquisitions editor at Libraries Unlimited, for believing in my project. Thanks also to Emma Bailey, production manager at Libraries Unlimited, for her help and expertise, and to Sue Stewart. I'd like to acknowledge the excellent staff at Publications Services, especially Susie Yates.

HOW TO USE THIS BOOK

Each section of *Quick and Easy Grammar Games to Boost Writing Power* follows a format that lends itself to today's standards-driven classroom while considering a teacher's busy schedule. You can modify activities for non-readers and writers by having students say instead of write the answers. They can also use motions, pantomime, gestures, drawings, and invented spelling to give responses. You can also change the small group activities to entire class sessions and have students speak rather than write the answers. If you have classes where some students can write, ask them to act as recorders for the small groups that include those who cannot write.

Home schooling parents will also find this book helpful as a supplementary English text. They can easily adapt the group and partnered activities to meet their individual needs.

The book's uniform format imparts a sense of order and direction to instruction, yet the activities are varied enough to maintain student interest and involvement. All of the activities comply with the National Council of Teachers of English and International Reading Association standards (NCTE/IRA), and state and local standards.

Each lesson begins with *Teacher Tips*, which provides a rationale for teaching a specific point of grammar as it relates to writing. The tips also give tested ideas for teaching each unit.

The *Pre-Game Activity* provides a warm-up for the games by introducing the various points of grammar using a multi-sensory approach, which appeals to a variety of learning styles.

A *Lesson Plan*, which features step-by-step instructions for a grammar game designed to build writing skills, follows. *Follow-Up Activities*, which help to solidify the skills learned in each game, include whole class, group, and partnered activities.

Homework includes an interesting reproducible activity to share with a parent, guardian, sibling, or other adult homework helper. You can use the *Practice* section for reviewing or testing the concepts studied in each lesson. Constructed for easy scoring, the multiple-choice questions provide an assessment or review tool for each lesson in the form of perforated, reproducible pages.

Finally, *Cumulative Writing Practice*, a review in the form of a writing assignment, wraps up each unit, stressing to students that grammar provides a means to the end of helping them become better writers, rather than being an end in itself. In addition, the *Cumulative Writing Practice* gives the student experience with all of the grammar lessons and helps students build upon previous lessons. This section includes assignments in each of the four writing domains: expressive, narrative, informational, and persuasive.

For students who are just learning to write, or for those whose writing skills are minimal, the teacher can use the writing practice and the cumulative writing practice as a homework assignment. The student can dictate ideas to the homework helper or use invented spelling.

To give students practice in self-editing, have them proofread their papers using the checklist in the appendix every time they write. As they learn new concepts, have them check their papers against new items on the list.

Make peer collaboration part of the editing process by having students consult with a student writing partner before writing their final drafts. Writing partners check the rough drafts against the writing checklist and then confer with each other and offer suggestions for revision. Pair students who can best benefit each other's writing progress. You may want to change partners periodically.

Encourage students to keep a writing portfolio where they will keep their grammar notes, practices, and writing assignments in chronological order. Teachers, parents, and homework helpers can check the student's writing progress by reviewing this folder.

UNIT 1

VERBS

STRONG ACTION VERBS

Teacher Tips

You can't have a sentence without a verb. Today most popular writing, including children's books, features strong action verbs. There is no place for sentences dominated by weak, wishy-washy verbs or linking verbs like *am, is,* or *was.* Help students create vivid pictures with their writing by teaching them how to use strong action verbs.

Write a list of linking verbs or the verb *be* (*am, is, are, was, were*) on the board. Talk about how students will need to use them sometimes, but that most of the time it's best to use strong action verbs.

Also, write passive voice sentences on the board and compare them to active voice sentences: for example, compare the active "Dr. Seuss wrote the story." to the passive "The story was written by Dr. Seuss." You don't have to say that the passive voice contains part of the verb *to be* plus the past participle of the main verb. It is enough at this stage to give examples and compare the active and passive voice, letting the evidence speak for itself. Ask students why they think it is better to use the active voice (it uses fewer words; it sounds better).

Game: Be the Strongest, Mightiest Verb You Can "Bee"

This game helps students differentiate between strong action verbs, weak linking verbs, and passive voice, and gives students the tools for writing more interesting and lively sentences.

Pre-Game Activity

1. Read the class a favorite picture book. As they identify the strong action verbs in the story, write them on the board.
2. Have student volunteers act out some of the verbs. Ask how a verb is different from the other words in a sentence. (It shows action.)
3. Write sentences from the story on the board, eliminating the verbs. Ask the students to discuss what is missing from each sentence and how it affects the meaning. (There's no action. The sentence doesn't make sense without action.) Discuss how action can also be mental instead of physical: *think, believe,* and *feel.*
4. Have the students brainstorm action verbs. Write them on the board and have them give sentences for each of the verbs. Ask them why it is good to use strong verbs when writing. (It makes sentences more interesting and helps the writer tell a better story.)

Lesson Plan

1. Stage a Verb Bee. Students form a line around the room as they would for a Spelling Bee. Each participant thinks of an action verb rather than a linking verb.
2. Write (or have a student write) the verbs on the board. The students continue to name strong action verbs until they can't think of any more and then sit down. The winner is left standing.
3. Sometimes we use verbs as nouns and vice versa, depending on the meaning in the sentence. Talk about how words can be used differently in sentences; sometimes they're action words (verbs), and other times they're nouns (people, places, or things). You can use some verbs in the practice exercise that follows (*coughs, smiles, sneezes*) as nouns. Have students give sentences using these words as action verbs and sentences using them as nouns. (Verb: The baby smiles when I tickle her. Noun: The clowns's smiles brightened up the room.) For the practice exercise, tell students to think of all action words as verbs.

Follow-Up (Poetry)

1. Have the students form groups. Give each group a card that contains five of the verbs the class gave in the verb bee. Ask each group to write a rhymed or unrhymed (free-verse) poem

about a noun (person, place, or thing) using the verbs on the cards. See the appendix for a discussion of poetry and suggested poems. Read rhymed and free-verse poems from children's and adult poetry anthologies aloud. Have the students explain the differences between free-verse and rhymed poetry. Talk about how free-verse poems don't rhyme but instead follow a natural rhythm. Student-written poems can be serious or funny. Have students underline the verbs.

2. Have each group read its poem to the class. Ask the class to identify at least three verbs in each poem.

3. Ask students to meet in their groups, rewrite their poems on good paper, and illustrate them for display. Have them highlight the verbs in yellow.

HOMEWORK

The homework helper sets a timer for five minutes, and the student thinks of as many strong action verbs as he or she can in the time allotted. The helper writes the verbs as the student dictates them. If the student has trouble thinking of verbs, the helper can help by acting out words or giving clues.

PRACTICE 1: STRONG ACTION VERBS

Circle the letter of the strong action verb. In the space below the words, write a sentence using all the words given. Feel free to change the order of the words in each question. To make your sentence more interesting, add more words (adjectives) to describe the noun (person, place, or thing). Add *a, and,* or *the* if it makes the sentence sound better. Score five points for each correct answer. Each sentence needs two answers: the letter of the action verb and a sentence.

1. a. dragon b. candy c. ate

   _____

   _____

2. a. burps b. zebra c. never

   _____

   _____

3. a. baby b. yawns c. the

   _____

   _____

4. a. teacher b. always c. smiles

   _____

   _____

5. a. coughs b. elephant c. the

   _____

   _____

6. a. clown b. chuckles c. never

   _____

   _____

7. a. sneezes b. reindeer c. often

   _____

   _____

8. a. Mom b. bridges c. builds

   _____

   _____

9. a. Grandmother b. bus c. drives

   _____

   _____

10. a. jogs b. father c. my

   _____

   _____

THE RIGHT VERB

| Teacher Tips |

The verbs we choose can make a difference between an ordinary sentence and a dazzling one. We can ask students to think about using the right verb to paint the perfect word picture.

If you had the choice between "The student *put* his backpack on the table*"* or "The student *slammed* his backpack on the table," which verb would you choose to show that the student was upset about something?

Using the right verb helps us show, rather than tell, what's happening. It helps create a word picture that will stay with the reader. Learning to choose verbs wisely helps students write more precisely and creatively.

We can make sentences come alive by using strong verbs. When we write, taking the time to find the perfect verb helps us paint a better picture of what we are trying to say.

| Game: Verbs Come in All Colors |

This game will give practice in generating synonyms for action verbs and choosing the best verb for a sentence. It will also provide practice for taking standardized tests, which require students to make the best choice.

| Pre-Game Activity |

1. Ask the class to look at the various shades of one color within their crayon or pencil boxes to see how the shades of a color make a difference in the picture they're coloring or drawing. For example, you can ask how royal blue differs from turquoise. How is robin's egg blue different from dark blue? When would it be better to choose one over another? (If you were painting a night sky, for example, you might choose violet or dark blue. If you were painting an ocean, you'd probably choose turquoise.)
2. Have students describe how the variations of a single color look different to them. Explain how we also paint pictures with the words we use and how changing the word to another word which means the same thing (synonym) can make a big difference in meaning. Here are some examples: the cat *meandered*, rather than *walked*; the dog *scampered*, rather than *ran*. As students give more examples, write them on the board.

| Lesson Plan |

1. Divide the class into groups. Assign each group an action word (examples: *talk, shout, jump, run*).
2. Ask each group to brainstorm as many synonyms for the verb as they can in a set amount of time. Have a class recorder write the verbs as students think of them.

3. When the time is up, ask each group to tell the class its verb and synonyms. Write them on the board and have students think of additional synonyms and add them to the list.

Follow-Up

1. Have students work in groups. Ask them to choose another group's word and to use each synonym for that word listed on the board in a sentence. Have them explain how the meanings vary as shades of a color vary.
2. Read the students a story and list some of the verbs in the story on the board. Reread each sentence with the listed verbs. Ask them why they think the author chose or didn't choose the best verb possible for the sentence. Why is it better to use one verb over another?
3. Have students meet with a partner. Ask them to choose two verbs from the story that you listed on the board and to think of at least two other verbs that mean the same thing. Have them write sentences for the verbs and draw a picture to illustrate the action. You may want to introduce the thesaurus or a children's thesaurus to older students at this point.

HOMEWORK

The homework helper reads a picture book and asks the student to describe at least five different actions in the story. Have the student list the verbs the author used and then think of other verbs to describe the same actions.

PRACTICE 2: THE RIGHT VERB

Fill in the verb that best fits the sentence. Choose the most colorful word, the word that makes you picture the action. Write the word in the space. Be ready to tell why you chose the answer you did. Which words in the sentence gave you clues about which word to use? Score 10 points for each correct answer.

1. The clown _____ (walked, tiptoed, raced) through the tulips so we couldn't hear him sneak up on us.

2. When I _____ (touched, stroked, patted) the kitten gently, he purred softly.

3. The gigantic spider _____ (scurried, crawled, ran) from the shower as soon as I went in.

4. The field mouse _____ (hopped, scampered, jumped) under the door when we tried to catch him.

5. My dog _____ (fetched, grabbed, caught) the meaty bone I threw her.

6. Mom _____ (mixed, baked, made) a chocolate cake with rainbow sprinkles for my birthday.

7. My grandfather _____ (chewed, ate, licked) the ice cream cone slowly because he loves mint chocolate chip.

8. Dad _____ (jogged, walked, skipped) around the block five times to work off the five pieces of pizza he ate.

9. The big pumpkin _____ (rolled, fell, moved) down the driveway, and turned into pumpkin pie.

10. We _____ (giggled, smiled, laughed) when our teacher told us a silly joke.

VERB TENSE: REGULAR VERBS

To write clearly, students need to know how to identify and use the simple tenses (present, past, and future). Learning how to use tenses correctly and consistently will help students impart a sense of order and logic to their writing. Read students a story and ask whether the story is happening now (present) or happened before (past). Have them tell something that could happen in the future if the story continued.

Game: My Dog _Barks_ Today, _Barked_ Yesterday, and _Will Bark_ Tomorrow

This game reviews the concepts of the present, past, and future tenses of regular verbs and provides practice for writing sentences using these tenses.

Pre-Game Activity

1. Pass out three three-by-five notecards to each student. Ask the students to write three sentences (one sentence to each three-by-five card). One sentence will tell about something they've enjoyed doing in the past, another will relate to something they're doing now, and a final sentence will describe something they'd like to do in the future.
2. Collect the cards and assign them randomly to class members. Have students read one of their classmate's sentences aloud. Ask the students to tell when the event happened and to tell how they know. Ask what clues they have that the event is happening now, happened before, or will happen. (They can identify the present tense ending, which is simply the verb in its basic form; the past tense, which ends in _ed_ for regular verbs; and the future tense, which is preceded by _will_.)
3. Call on another student to change the sentence to a different tense. Ask a classmate to identify it as present, past, or future tense.

Lesson Plan

1. The class will work in groups. Assign each group a regular action verb ending in _d_ or _ed_. Instead of assigning an ordinary verb, you may want to give each group a category like animal noises (_bark, quack, honk_), people's actions (_snore, yawn, stretch_), or people's facial expressions (_frown, squint, laugh_).
2. Focusing on this verb, have students make up a colorful chart with illustrations listing the action verb in the present, past, and future tenses. Post the charts and tell the students to look at all of them in the next day or so.

3. After they've had a chance to see the verb charts, have students form groups. They will write a sentence for another group's verbs using each of the tenses. They will label the verbs *present*, *past*, and *future*.

4. When the groups complete the work, have a member of each group quiz the class on whether the verb used in each sentence is in the present, past, or future tense.

Follow-Up

1. Ask students to write brief stories about something they did in the past, something they are doing in the present, or something they hope to do in the future. Have them read their stories to the class. Ask the class to determine whether most of the action occurs in the present, past, or future tense. Ask the class to give examples of the main tense used in each story. Write the words on the board and have students identify the tense as present, past, or future.

2. Ask students to construct a timeline of major events in their lives (for example, year of birth, year started school, year beginning a hobby or sport, future dream job, future place of residence) using the three categories of past, present, and future tense. Then ask them to use the timeline to write a paragraph about one of the events. Have them attach the story to the timeline and make up an original title for the paragraph relating to time or tense.

3. Have students take turns reading their narratives to the class. Ask the class: "What clues do you have that the event is happening now, happened before, or will happen?"

HOMEWORK

The homework helper has the student write two sentences about something exciting he or she did in the past, in the present, and something he or she hopes to do in the future. Students will underline the verb in the present tense, circle the verb ending for the past tense, and draw a box around the future tense.

From *Quick and Easy Grammar Games to Boost Writing Power*. Copyright © 2006 by Catherine DePino. Westport, CT: Teacher Ideas Press/Libraries Unlimited.

PRACTICE 3: VERB TENSE

Circle *a* or *b* for the correct verb for each sentence. Write present, past, or future in the space at the end of the sentence to show the verb tense. Which clues in the sentence helped you choose the right verb? (Score five points for each correct answer. Each sentence needs two answers.)

1. My brother _____ the drums every night after I go to sleep.
   (a. played b. plays) _____

2. The teacher _____ the gerbil if it escapes from the cage. (a. will chase b. chased)_____

3. My friend and I _____ when the cat ate the tuna Mom had made for our lunch. (a. laugh b. laughed) _____

4. My cousin and I _____an ice igloo in the yard the next time it snows.
   (a. will build b. built) _____

5. Mom _____ into my room and said it looked like a big storm hit it. (a. will walk b. walked) _____

6. The students _____ tag in the schoolyard if it does not rain.
   (a. will play b. played) _____

7. Emily _____ the ball into the basket and scored three points.
   (a. tossed b. toss) _____

8. John _____ chocolate chip cookies for the school party next week. (a. baked b. will bake) _____

9. The baby _____ me to play with him every time he sees me.
   (a. wants b. wanted) _____

10. I _____ the lemon pie, and it made my mouth pucker.(a. taste b. tasted) _____

VERB TENSE: IRREGULAR VERBS

Teacher Tips

It's sometimes a challenge for students to grasp the concept of irregular verbs. If it's all right to say I *baked* a cake, why can't I say I *builded* a snowman? The best way to learn irregular verbs is to see them, say them, and work with them until they become a part of everyday speech and writing.

It's important to show how irregular verbs look and sound different from regular verbs in the past tense and past participle (*has* and *have* forms). We will concentrate on the helping verbs *have, has*, and *had* as part of the past participle, even though participial forms are also used with other helping verbs (parts of the verb *to be* as in *were broken*).

Ask students how most verbs end when you're talking about something that happened in the past (*ed* and *d* as in *cooked, smiled*). Point out how some verbs may change into a completely different word for the past tense (*swim, swam, have swum*). There are a few verbs that do not change at all in the past tense (*beat, beat*) and some that do not change in the past tense and past participle (*burst, burst, burst*). All of these verbs are irregular verbs. Each forms its past tense and past participles in a different way.

Game: I (Seen) No! *Saw* the Squirrel Fall Off the Seesaw

This game explains the differences between regular and irregular verbs and gives examples of each. It helps attune the ear to proper verb usage.

Pre-Game Activity

1. Reproduce the list of commonly used irregular verbs (see appendix). Ask how irregular verbs look different from regular verbs. (They don't end in *d* or *ed* as regular verbs do. Sometimes they form a completely different word.)
2. Ask the class to think of additional verbs they think may be irregular because they don't use *d* or *ed* for the past tense. Write these words on the board and have students add them to their lists.
3. Have students read the past, present, and past participles of the irregular verbs individually and then chorally as a group.
4. Ask each student to meet with a partner to write sentences using the irregular verbs on the list. Have them highlight the verbs. Ask partners to read their sentences to the class, write their words on the board, and explain why they are irregular verbs

Lesson Plan

1. Have students brainstorm examples of outrageous irregular verb use they've heard.

Examples: past tense: brang, seen, runned
Examples: past participle: have/has ate;
have/has bursted; have/has froze

---

2. Write the bloopers on the board as the students dictate them. If you think this activity is too difficult for your class, you may want to present a list of verb bloopers (see appendix) and ask students to give the correct verb forms.
3. Have the class form groups and ask them to write four humorous sentences reflecting mistakes they've heard people make using irregular verbs. Tell them to refer to the list of verbs used in the first activity. Have them underline the verb errors and write the correct verb forms above the mistakes.
4. Ask each group to write its most humorous sentence with a verb blooper on the board. Class members will correct the errors orally and on the board, crossing out the errors and replacing them with proper verb forms. The entire class will vote on the silliest sentence using a verb blooper.

Follow-Up

1. Have students meet in groups. Referring to their lists of irregular verbs, they will write a story about going on an adventure to find a hidden treasure. Ask them to use at least four irregular verbs in the past tense or the past participle (*has* and *have* form) in the story and to highlight them.
2. Have a student from each group read its story to the class. Ask class members to identify the irregular verbs in each story and to give the three principal parts of at least two irregular verbs from each story.

HOMEWORK

Write the present tense of common irregular verbs on index cards. Take turns drawing cards. The homework helper and student will write or say sentences using the past tense and past participle of the irregular verbs on the cards. They will verify answers by referring to the original list. Check that each sentence contains a complete thought.

From *Quick and Easy Grammar Games to Boost Writing Power.* Copyright © 2006 by Catherine DePino. Westport, CT: Teacher Ideas Press/Libraries Unlimited.

PRACTICE 4: IRREGULAR VERBS

Write the letter of the correct answer, choosing the correct past tense or past participle (*has, have* form) of the irregular verb. Score 10 points for each correct answer.

1. The elephant has _____ her baby how to eat a peanut with her trunk. (a. teached b. taught)

2. We _____ in the pool after we toasted marshmallows. (a. swam b. swimmed)

3. My sister _____ the balloon, and I jumped in the air like a flea. (a. bursted b. burst)

4. I _____ a firefly, and it lit up on my arm. (a. caught b. catched)

5. I have _____ two pitchers of pink lemonade at my stand. (a. sold b. selled)

6. Mom _____ cupcakes with pink icing to school for our party. (a. bringed b. brought)

7. I have_____ all my dinner, and I will have a brownie for dessert. (a. ate b. eaten)

8. Michael has _____ a homework pass instead of popcorn for his prize. (a. chosen b. chose)

9. The teacher has _____to Amanda many times about letting the hamster out of the cage. (a. spoke b. spoken)

10. Grandmom said, "My, how you have _____ like a beanstalk!" (a. grew b. grown)

From Quick and Easy Grammar Games to Boost Writing Power. Copyright © 2006 by Catherine DePino. Westport, CT: Teacher Ideas Press/Libraries Unlimited.

> Writing Practice: Learn How to Write a Paragraph. Write Better Paragraphs With Strong Verbs.

One of the goals of this book is to help students learn how to write a good paragraph about any topic. For the first major assignment, students will write a one paragraph personal narrative about one of these three topics: friends, pets, or hobbies. As an in-class assignment, ask them to write a topic sentence and at least three supporting details in a brief outline.

Instead of writing a formal outline, they can put numbers in front of the main points they will cover in their paragraphs. (See appendix for a sample outline.) Every time they write, they will use this simple phrase outline form to plan their writing. They will write their topic sentence and, after they compose their outline, their ending sentence.

Have students check their outlines to make sure the order of their ideas makes sense. If not, they can juggle the order of the numbers in front of the details to help create a more logical, organized story. Have students write a brief word or phrase outline before they begin every writing assignment. Remind them to be sure that every detail supports the topic sentence and that one follows another in a good order.

Students can use one type of supporting detail or a combination to develop their paragraphs. They can use sensory details (which employ sight, sound, taste, smell, and texture) to liven up the subject. They can use examples, an anecdote (story), or facts. Show students examples of passages in a social studies textbook; have them state the topic sentence and the type or types of supporting details in a paragraph from the textbook.

Before students put their stories together, ask them what kinds of words they would use to join their different ideas together in a paragraph. If they mention words like *also*, *but*, and *however*, they're telling you they would use transitions. You might want to call a transition a smooth move to the next sentence. Students don't necessarily have to use transitions to link sentences as long as their ideas follow a logical order.

They will write their rough drafts in class, asking for help from you or a class writing partner if they need it. For this assignment, tell them to highlight the strong action verbs they use. They will also label at least four action verbs in their paragraphs, writing *present* above a present tense verb, *past* above a past tense verb, and *future* above a future tense verb. After following their plan for the story, they will add a closing sentence and an interesting title.

Before students write their final drafts for each unit, duplicate and distribute the writing checklist from the appendix, telling them which points to use as a basis for evaluating each writing practice. Students will refer to the checklist as they proofread their writing.

Writing partners will also use the checklist to offer suggestions to improve their partner's writing.

Students will meet with their writing partners to discuss ideas for revision of each other's paragraphs. They will look at the verbs used, at how the paragraph flows, and at the beginning and ending sentences. They will offer suggestions to their partner for improving the final draft.

Students will take their partner's ideas into consideration when writing their final copies, but they will ultimately decide what corrections they will make. Have partners write their names on each other's papers along with their suggestions so that you can evaluate the types of comments they made.

View selected student stories with an overhead projector. Ask students to comment on the suitability of the verbs used. Would they suggest others? Why?

Ask them to identify the topic sentence and supporting details. Have them determine whether the paragraph is too short or too long. What do they need to do to make it a better paragraph?

Ask the class to examine the story for a logical progression of ideas (beginning, middle, and end) and for an interesting title. Have them offer suggestions to improve the stories.

UNIT

2

LINKING VERBS

Explain that while linking verbs don't show any actions that we can see, they relate one word to another in the sentence. In the sentence "Ruff is my dog," the linking verb *is* links the word *Ruff* to *dog*. There is action in the sense that it reflects a state of being or something that's happening.

You might explain the action a linking verb shows in this way: If someone is sitting in a chair or even sleeping, there's something going on in that she's breathing, her brain is working, her body's doing all the things it has to do to keep going—whether she's thinking about it or not.

We need the linking verbs, or parts of the verb *to be* (*am, is, are, was, were, be*, and *being*) to complete some sentences, but when we can, it's best to use action verbs to make our sentences lively and interesting.

Some additional linking verbs (*grow, feel, look, smell, sound,* and *taste*, to name a few) can pose problems for students because they're harder to identify. Sometimes the same linking verb can show up in a sentence as an action verb (I tasted the soup.), and another time as a linking verb (The soup tasted delicious.).

In the first instance, I am actively tasting the soup. You can picture me doing it, so it's an action verb. In the second, *tasted* links *soup* with the adjective *delicious*, and nothing is happening that you can see. Therefore, tasted is a linking verb in the second example.

Game: Linking Verbs are Everywhere!

This game shows the difference between action and linking verbs in a sentence and gives examples of when to use linking verbs.

Pre-Game Activity

1. Review the linking verbs from the teacher tips section of this unit. Also discuss the other linking verbs (*taste, smell, feel,* etc.) that can be either linking or action verbs, depending on their use in the sentence. Have students write their own sentences on the board, underlining the linking verbs.

2. After students write the sentences, ask how linking verbs differ from action verbs (they don't show action you can see). Ask how they can help in writing and how they might not help. On the positive side, linking verbs can help describe people, places, and things in a sentence. On the negative side, you can't see anything happening as you can with action verbs. Linking verbs don't create a vivid picture of the action as action verbs do.

3. List the second type of linking verbs that you can use as a linking or an action verb (*feel, look, smell, sound, taste*). Have students take turns thinking of sentences using these words as linking and action verbs (see examples in the appendix). Have them explain the difference in meaning. Ask volunteers to act out the verbs when they're used as action verbs. Ask what happens when they try to act out the verbs used as linking verbs. (They won't be able to because there's no action you can see.)

Lesson Plan

1. Have students meet with partners. Ask them to interview each other and to give answers to the questions using linking verbs. Each team will write six sentences. Here are some examples of questions: What is your name? Use three words to describe yourself. Name and describe a person in your family. Tell what kind of work the person does.
   Write at least one sentence using a linking verb telling about something that happened before. Write at least one sentence telling about something that will happen in the future.

Example (present tense): I *am* a softball player.
　Example (past tense): My sister *was* in middle school last year.
　Example (future tense): My uncle *will be* in high school next year.

2. Have volunteers conduct their interviews for the class. Ask the class to listen and record the verbs used. Ask them to identify

the linking verbs and tell whether they are in the present, past, or future tense.

Follow-Up

1. Have students meet in groups. Give each group a slip of paper with a word they can use as a linking verb or an action verb. Have students make up two sentences using their word as a linking verb and two sentences using the word as an action verb. Refer to the model sentences in the appendix.
2. Ask the group members or a group chairperson to take turns reading sentences to the entire class. Have the class determine whether the verb is used as a linking verb or an action verb, and have the groups verify answers.

HOMEWORK

Have the student make up interview questions for you using linking verbs. The student will also answer the questions.

Examples: What is your favorite food? What was your favorite subject when you were in school? What were your friends' names?

Answer the questions and have the student say or write the linking verbs you both used. Have the student experiment with changing around the word order in the sentences: My favorite food is crab.; Crab is my favorite food.

ALTERNATE HOMEWORK ASSIGNMENT (ADVANCED)

Review the verbs that you can use as linking or action verbs (*feel, look, sound, smell,* and *taste*). Have students write and act out a sentence for each verb used as an action verb. Have them say or write sentences for the same verbs used as linking verbs. Ask which words the verbs link. (In the sentence, "My cat feels furry," *feels* links *cat* with *furry.*)

PRACTICE 5: LINKING VERBS

Underline the linking verb in sentences 1-5. For sentences 6-10, write *L* if the verb in dark print is used as a linking verb. Write *A* if it is used as an action verb.

1. Jade was a big pumpkin for the costume party.

2. The children were happy playing in the mud.

3. Are you the student who made a home run?

4. My cat's name is Clarabel.

5. I am full after eating two pieces of chocolate pie.

6. **Feel** the dog's nose to see if she's healthy.

7. The bean soup **tastes** spicy.

8. Do you **smell** the burnt toast?

9. **Look** at the dog eating a hamburger.

10. Mom said that my music **sounds** too loud.

Cumulative Writing Practice: Describe a Favorite Food or Meal Using Linking Verbs

Have students write a paragraph describing a favorite food or meal. Have them use at least three linking verbs, including ones like *taste*, *smell*, and *look*, which they can use as linking or action verbs. Tell them to underline the linking verbs and to circle the linking verbs used as action verbs.

Remind them to outline their paragraphs with at least three points to support the main idea, to use transitions or smooth moves to the next sentence (when they can), and to think of an interesting beginning and conclusion. Ask volunteers to read their paragraphs to the class and to read a sentence using a verb that can either be a linking or an action verb. Ask the class to explain why the verbs are considered linking or action verbs in each case.

COMMON NOUNS AND PROPER NOUNS

Teacher Tips

Start teaching the noun by defining it as a person, place, or thing. Explain the difference between common and proper nouns, give examples, and ask for student examples.

Everything we see, hear, or touch is a noun. Nouns, along with verbs, form the backbone of sentences. Help students learn the importance of using strong, specific nouns rather than dragging down their sentences with too many adjectives.

Game: Nouns Can Be Ordinary, or Prim and Proper

This game helps students differentiate between common and proper nouns.

Pre-Game Activity

1. Discuss the definition of nouns. Write class examples on the board as they list common nouns to represent people, places, or things. Have them think of proper nouns related to each common noun.

Examples: common noun-**person**: woman; proper noun-**person**: Amanda; common noun-**place**: city; proper noun-**place**: Honolulu; common noun-**thing**: car; proper noun-**thing**: SUV

2. Have students work with a partner. Ask students to divide a sheet of lined paper into three parts using a ruler. Use *person*, *place*, and *thing* as the headings. Have them think of at least five examples of common nouns for each category.

3. Ask partners to give examples to the class without saying which category (person, place, or thing) their nouns represent. Class members will identify the categories of the nouns as students name them. Write selected student examples for each category on the board.

4. Have students write or draw (in class or for homework) two examples of proper nouns for each type of noun.

5. Ask the class to share examples of proper nouns that relate to common nouns.

Lesson Plan

1. Ask students to write a fiction or non-fiction story (explain the difference) on a topic of their choice, focusing on one type of noun: person, place, or thing. They should use at least three common and two proper nouns in the story. Ask them to highlight every example of the type of noun used.

2. Look at sample stories on the overhead projector. Ask the class to identify common and proper nouns from the underlined words. As they give their answers, write *C* above the common nouns and *P* above the proper nouns.

3. Have other volunteers read or tell the class their stories. Ask the class whether they think the stories are fiction or non-fiction and why they think so. Ask the stories' creators to verify answers.

Follow-Up

1. Have students work with a partner. Ask them to list ten common nouns. Ask them to write whether each noun is a person, place, or thing.

2. Have students report their findings to the class without divulging the category of each noun. Write the nouns on the board and have the class tell why each word is a noun (is it a person, place, or thing?).

3. Divide the class into teams. Have team members take turns giving proper nouns related to the common nouns on the board. (Examples: person: teacher, Mr. Diggs; place: school, Carver Elementary School; thing: car, Ford.)

HOMEWORK

The student and homework helper go on a treasure hunt inside of or outside of the house to find three examples of people, places, and things. They will make a chart with the three categories and will write three common nouns and one related proper noun for each of the three categories. The next day students will report their findings to the class.

PRACTICE 6: COMMON AND PROPER NOUNS

Underline the common nouns once and the proper nouns twice. Each sentence has two nouns. A noun may have more than one word if it is closely related. Score five points for each correct answer.

1. The airplane zoomed across New York.

2. Mr. Plunket teaches violin.

3. My mother drove to Kalamazoo.

4. Mrs. Pringle works as a clown.

5. We ate popcorn at the Princeton Mall.

6. Is that Lincoln on the money?

7. We bought an apple cake at The Cake Factory.

8. I saw an alligator in Florida.

9. The seagull swam across the Atlantic Ocean.

10. I named my mouse Mr. Cheese Please.

THE BEST NOUN

Teacher Tips

Just as your students should use the best verb in writing, it's also important to consider which noun works best. When relating nouns to writing, advise students to use specific, rather than general nouns. Readers can more easily picture a Greyhound rather than a dog or a cottage rather than a house.

Sometimes sentences need adjectives to clarify meaning; other times it's enough to use a specific noun. As you read stories to your class, point out examples of specific nouns. Have students tell why using that noun is better than using a more general one.

Cutting down on the excess words in sentences and streamlining them promotes clarity and better reading comprehension. Ask students to zero in on the more precise word rather than using a broader, more general term.

Examples: cat (general), Tabby (specific); instrument (general), drum (specific).

Game: Search for the Perfect Noun

This game helps students learn the difference between general and specific nouns and how to use nouns to their best advantage in writing.

Pre-Game Activity

1. Have the students meet in groups. Give each group a noun representing a general category (examples: sports, clothes, desserts, toys). Ask them to make up a list of nouns that would fit their category (for example, dessert: cake, pie, ice cream, cookie, candy, pretzels). They can use common or proper nouns. If you want, make it a contest. The group that lists the most nouns wins.
2. Ask each group to write or tell their main noun and the nouns they listed under it. See if the class can come up with more nouns.

Lesson Plan

1. Ask the groups to pretend they're going to open a store selling a certain product (for example, a bakery, restaurant, pet store, toy store, or clothing store). Assign or discuss topics to be sure there's no overlap. Tell them not to use adjectives for this exercise—only nouns.
2. Have each group make up a booklet listing products they'll sell at their store. Ask them to illustrate the booklet with colorful drawings. Have them write C above the common nouns and P above the proper nouns they list. Encourage students to make up their own brand names rather than using ones they've seen.

Examples: (bakery) donuts-common noun, Dunker Delight-proper noun; (pet store) dog-common noun, Collie-proper noun; (toy store) bubbles-common noun; Bubblemania-proper noun

3. Ask group spokespersons to talk about their products and to tell why they're nouns.
4. Post the booklets in the hall for other classes to see. Your class may want to describe their stores to another class and explain why using specific nouns in writing is important.

Follow-Up

1. Have groups write and illustrate an ad for their stores, inviting people to buy their products. Ask them to highlight all nouns with a yellow highlighter and to write *C* and *P* above the common and proper nouns.
2. Ask all students in the group to proofread the ads and to add suggestions before they write their final copy.
3. Have students present their ads to the class, asking classmates to shop in their stores.

HOMEWORK

Have the student go to at least three different rooms in the house and find six examples of common nouns. Now have the student turn all the examples into proper nouns (for example, common noun: sister, proper noun: Tamika; common noun: cat, proper noun: Whiskers; common noun: book, proper noun: *Treasure Island*).

PRACTICE 7: SPECIFIC NOUNS

Read both pairs of sentences. Circle the letter of the sentence with the specific noun. Be ready to discuss why the specific noun sounds better.

1. (a) I gave Mom flowers for her birthday.
   (b) I gave Mom roses for her birthday.

2. (a) Look at that Dalmatian in the window.
   (b) Look at that puppy in the window.

3. (a) Melissa wore her new outfit to the party.
   (b) Melissa wore her new dress to the party.

4. (a) Lamont brought sandwiches to the picnic.
   (b) Lamont brought food to the picnic.

5. (a) The baby played with the toy.
   (b) The baby played with the jack-in-the-box.

6. (a) Juan plays sports after school.
   (b) Juan plays hockey after school.

7. (a) A mouse crawled into my sleeping bag.
   (b) A creature crawled into my sleeping bag.

8. (a) We went out for dessert.
   (b) We went out for milkshakes.

9. (a) The chef made seafood for dinner.
   (b) The chef made fried snails for dinner.

10. (a) The animal flashed his teeth at me.
    (b) The gorilla flashed his teeth at me.

Cumulative Writing Practice: Write a Poem Using Nouns

Review the appendix (Unit 1, Follow-Up, Poetry) for information about free-verse and rhymed poetry. Have students bring in their favorite poems. Read or have students read them to the class. Ask the class if they are free-verse or rhymed poems and have them tell why.

Have students work independently. They will write free-verse or rhymed poems of at least five lines on one of the following topics: special holidays, interesting relatives, or places they've been. They will use at least four common and two proper nouns. Have them label common nouns *C* and proper nouns *P*.

Have students draw illustrations to accompany their poems. Ask students to read their poems aloud to the class. After each reading, ask the class to identify the common and proper nouns from the poems. Display the poems.

UNIT

4

PRONOUNS

In this unit students will learn how to substitute pronouns for nouns. They will also see that some pronouns describe nouns. Students will learn about personal, possessive, interrogative, and demonstrative pronouns. You may want to simplify terms by calling interrogative pronouns, *pronouns that ask a question,* and demonstrative pronouns, *pronouns that point out.*

Game: Write a Riddle Using Pronouns

This game teaches different types of pronouns and their uses in sentences.

Pre-Game Activity

Allow at least one day to teach each type of pronoun.

1a. List the personal pronouns (*I, you, he, she, it, we, they*) on the board. List and discuss the objective case of personal pronouns (*me, you, him, her, it, us, them*). You don't have to call it objective case. Instead, you can say that they're different forms of the pronouns you've learned, and give sentence examples.

1b. You can also teach possessive pronouns (*my, your, his, hers, its, our, their*) since they fall under the banner of personal pronouns. Point out that you can use possessive pronouns before a noun to tell something about the noun, or that you can use them in place of a noun.

Examples: (Before a noun) Her pony won the race.
(In place of a noun) The winning pony is hers.

Have students give examples of all of these pronouns in sentences.

1c. Ask volunteers to take turns demonstrating each personal pronoun (*I, you, he, she, it, we, they*) by using gestures (see appendix). Have the class identify each pronoun.

1d. Ask students to work in groups. Assign each group a personal and a possessive pronoun. Have them make up a story that describes a person, place, or thing using their pronouns. Have them read it to the class. Ask the class to identify each group's personal pronouns.

2a. Ask students what the pronouns *who, whose, which*, and *what* have in common (they all ask a question).

2b. Students will work with a partner. Have them interview each other, asking questions about one of the following topics: places you go, people you see, games you play, music you hear (for example, Who is your best friend?; Whose cooking do you like?; Which game do you like playing?; Who is your favorite singer?).

2c. Have them write out the questions, leaving enough space for each answer. After answering the question they can write the answers in one or two sentences. They can exchange papers and discuss one another's answers.

3a. Write the demonstrative pronouns or pronouns that point out (*this, that, these*, and *those*) on the board. Ask a volunteer to explain how to use demonstrative pronouns using props like books or school supplies (see appendix). Also discuss how to use these pronouns as adjectives, or words that describe nouns (the topic of the next unit). Relate this to your discussion of using possessive pronouns as adjectives (see 1(b) in this section). It will help you reinforce the idea of determining the part of speech by its use in a sentence.

3b. Ask partners to write four sentences about a person, place, or thing, using each of the demonstrative pronouns. Have them think about the difference in meaning between *this, that, these*, and *those*. *This* and *these* refer to something near, while *that* and *those* refer to something farther away (see appendix).

Lesson Plan

1. Have the class get into groups. Provide them with a list of the four types of pronouns or write them on the board. Ask them to compose riddles of three sentences, using at least two pronouns. First they will write the riddle question using an

interrogative pronoun: for example, Who am I?; What is it?; Which student am I? A three-sentence riddle for the last question might be: I sit in the third row. You can find me on the baseball field. My hair is red.

2. Ask students to label the pronouns they used in their questions and answers by type, using these abbreviations: *P*, personal; *PQ*, pronouns that question; *POS*, possessive pronouns; *PPO*, pronouns that point out.

3. Have a person in each group read the riddles to the class. Ask the students to figure out the answers. Verify the answers with the group that composed the riddle. Have the class identify the pronouns and check the answers with the group that composed the riddle.

| Follow-Up |

1. Ask the class to brainstorm reasons for using pronouns. Answers may include the following: they point out things, they help us ask questions, they show that someone owns something, and they give us other ways to name people, animals, and things so that we're not always using the same words.

HOMEWORK

The student thinks of a person, place, or thing familiar to the homework helper and writes a question and several statements. For example: Who likes carrots but doesn't like peas? She is eight and lives next door. We see her once a week. Have the student circle the pronouns and tell what type they are. The helper names the person, place, or thing, and checks the student's answers.

PRACTICE 8: PRONOUNS

Circle the two pronouns in each sentence. Score five points for each correct answer.

1. What is that slimy blob in the ocean?

2. Do you see it crawling onto the sand?

3. I see my sister Anne walking toward the creature.

4. Which of us is brave enough to touch the sea monster?

5. She won't go near it.

6. My father looks at its flabby jelly body.

7. "This is a jelly fish, not a monster," he says.

8. Mom points to more jellyfish. "Those must be its friends."

9. "They are not our friends," Anne says.

10. "We should leave them alone to play," Mom says.

Cumulative Writing Practice: Write About an Interesting Place Using Strong Verbs, Specific Nouns, and Pronouns

Using strong verbs, specific nouns, and at least four pronouns, write a story about an interesting place you've visited. Underline and label all pronouns: **P,** personal, **PQ,** pronouns that question, **POS,** possessive pronouns, and **PPO,** pronouns that point out. Students will exchange papers with writing partners, who will check that pronouns are labeled correctly and will offer suggestions for revision.

UNIT
5
ADJECTIVES

Tell the students that an adjective used in the right place can make writing more interesting and descriptive. On the other hand, writing with too many descriptive words often lacks energy and slows the writing down.

Game: Play Adjective Round Robin

This game helps students identify and use adjectives to describe nouns in sentences. It encourages students to use creativity and figurative language in descriptions.

Pre-Game Activity

(Like some of the other lessons, this may span several days.)

1a. Tell students that *a*, *an*, and *the* are three adjectives they use every day. *A* and *an* must be used with certain types of nouns (*a* baseball, *an* orange). The first letter sound of the noun gives a good clue about which adjective to use.

1b. Review vowel and consonant sounds. Ask students to listen to examples of words beginning with these different sounds.

Examples of Words Beginning with Vowel Sounds: ape, egg, elephant, igloo

Examples of Words Beginning with Consonant Sounds: tadpole, turtle, foot, storm

1c. Ask students to give their own examples of words beginning with consonant and vowel sounds. Have other class members repeat the initial sounds of the nouns given. Ask them which adjective (*a* or *an*) they would use with each noun. Ask them when they would use *the* with the nouns (use *the* with nouns beginning with a vowel or consonant).

1d. Tell students to use *an* before words beginning with a vowel sound and *a* before words beginning with a consonant sound. Use *the* with words beginning with vowel or consonant sounds.

1e. Students will work with partners. Ask them to divide their paper into three columns and to head the first with *a*, the second with *an*, and the third with *the*. Ask them to pair each adjective with a noun that begins with the correct vowel or consonant sound. For *the*, they can use words beginning with vowel or consonant sounds. Ask volunteers to read their adjective/noun combinations to the class. Have the class tell why the adjective preceding the noun is correct or incorrect.

2a. Discuss how descriptive adjectives describe nouns or pronouns. Read students a story and point out how adjectives describe nouns. Have students give more examples from the story.

2b. Write a list of adjectives on the board to describe today's weather (*bright, overcast, sunny, cloudy, rainy, misty, foggy, snowy*). Ask students to think of their own adjectives and to tell why they think their word best describes the day.

3a. Have students get into groups. Ask them to divide a paper into three parts with these headings: *person*, *place*, and *thing*. Ask them to write a noun (common or proper) under each heading. They will brainstorm at least six adjectives to describe the noun they chose for each heading. Then they will put a star next to the one adjective under each heading that they think best describes the noun.

Example:

Person: teacher	Place: amusement park	Thing: costume
smart	gigantic	funny
strict	exciting	scary
caring	relaxing	colorful*
warm*	thrilling*	unusual
cheerful	happy	ugly
interesting	noisy	fancy

3b. Ask a person from each group to name the best adjective that describes each noun. Have the class discuss which one of the three top choices they like best and to explain why.

| Lesson Plan |

1. Have students sit in a circle. Draw three columns on the board, heading them with the words *person*, *place*, and *thing*. Ask the class to think of a noun to fill in each of the categories, or assign one.
2. Going around the circle, ask each student to name a descriptive adjective for the first category. Record all the adjectives on the board. If a student can't think of one, go to the next student. Do the same thing with the next two categories. Keep track of the student who scores the most points by giving the most answers. That student is the winner.
3. Ask the students to vote on the three best adjectives listed for each category.
4. Have the students write sentences using the three best adjectives in each category. Tell them to underline the adjective and circle the noun the adjective modifies.

| Follow-Up |

1. Have students work in pairs. Provide them with storybooks or readers. Ask them to copy five sentences that they think use good descriptive adjectives. They will underline the adjectives and circle the nouns they describe.
2. Ask students to rewrite the sentences using their own adjectives. Have volunteers read the originals and their revised sentences to the entire class.

HOMEWORK

Have your family sit around the table. Ask the student to think of a noun. Everyone (including the student) takes a turn thinking of an adjective to describe the noun and keeps going around the table until the last person remains. The student records everyone's adjective. If a person can't think of one, he or she is eliminated from the game and must leave the table. The last person left sitting is the winner. The student chooses the adjective he or she thinks best describes the noun and explains why.

PRACTICE 9: ADJECTIVES

Write a descriptive adjective for the nouns in dark print. If you see *a/an*, it means you can use a descriptive adjective that goes with *a* or *an*. Score ten points for each correct answer.

1. The _____ **soda** spilled on the table.

2. Chase ate a _____ **sandwich**.

3. Aisha played in the _____ **pool**.

4. The _____ **cat** tried to jump in the goldfish bowl.

5. Juan watched a/an _____ **cartoon**.

6. Would you like to eat a _____ **bowl** of turtle soup?

7. I love to watch a/an _____ **game**.

8. We planted _____ **flowers** in the garden.

9. Our teacher gave us a/an _____ **book** to read.

10. I took a picture of the _____ **rainbow**.

Cumulative Writing Practice: Describe Something in Nature Using Adjectives

Ask students to write a descriptive paragraph about something in nature. Have them use at least five descriptive adjectives and four articles. Have them label the descriptive adjectives *D* and the articles *A*. Ask them to think about whether the sentence would sound better with or without a descriptive adjective. Discuss sample sentences in class, using an overhead to view paragraphs.

UNIT
6
ADVERBS

Teacher Tips

When teaching adverbs, remind students that adverbs have their place in writing, but that they should think before using them in writing. The same advice that you gave about adjectives applies to adverbs. Writers sometimes overuse adverbs, making their writing sound heavy and clouding their message.

Adverbs modify verbs, adjectives, or other adverbs. They answer the questions *where, when, how,* and *to what extent* (how much). Sometimes adverbs end in *ly*, but not always.

Remind students that the parts of speech are determined by how the words are used in a sentence. For example, *tomorrow* is usually a noun, but in the sentence, "We will go to the play tomorrow," it is an adverb that tells when. Every time you explain a new part of speech, ask students to give examples using the same word as a different part of speech.

Game: Act Out Adverbs

This game teaches students how to identify and use adverbs wisely in sentences. It also reviews the major parts of speech.

Pre-Game Activity

1a. Explain that adverbs tell something more about verbs. (They also describe adjectives and other adverbs.) Adverbs answer the questions *where, when, how,* and *to what extent* (how much).

Examples: I ran *ahead*. (tells where)

49

I went to school *early.* (tells when)
Talk *quietly* in your groups. (tells how)
I walked *far.* (tells how much).

1b. Write the four headings (*where, when, how, how much*) that adverbs address on the board. Use these model sentences or write your own and place them under their respective headings. Ask students to complete the sentences with adverbs that answer the questions. Students will probably see adverbs used more in the first three situations; however, you'll want to show all the uses of adverbs as you introduce them.

Sample Sentences	Suggested Answers
Where: The kitten slept _____ .	here
When: I woke up_____ .	early
How: My dog barked_____ .	loudly
How Much: I _____ slept last night.	hardly

1c. Have students work with a partner. Ask them to write a sentence for each of the four types of adverbs: those that tell *where, when, how,* or *how much.* Have them circle the verb, underline the adverb, and write the question the adverb answers above it.

1d. Ask volunteers to read sentences to the entire class, stating the adverb and the verb it modifies. Have class members judge whether the words they have used are adverbs and whether the students used them in the manner described.

Lesson Plan

1. Ask students to meet in groups. Have them think of ways they can act out four adverbs of their choice, using two word command sentences (for example, *sing loudly; speak softly; walk slowly; leave early*). One or more students in the group will present the sentences to the class.

2. After writing the sentence minus the adverb on the board, have students act out the adverbs for the class. The class tries to figure out the adverb, and the presenting group verifies the answer.

3. The class writes their own sentences using adverbs, expanding the sentences to include limiting and descriptive adjectives.

Examples: The rock star sings *loudly.*; The shy student spoke *softly.;* The big turtle walked *slowly.;* The bored girl left *early.*

4. Class members will share their sentences, identifying the parts of speech learned so far (noun, verb, adjective, adverb).

Follow-Up

1. Students will work in pairs to make a diagram of two or three adverbs that modify one verb. Assign the verb or give students a choice of verbs from a story they've read. Have them circle a verb and cluster adverbs they might use with that verb. They will use arrows to create circles that spring out of the verb and write adverbs in the circles that would fit that verb.

Example:

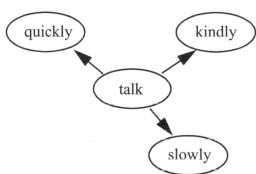

2. Have students present their cluster diagrams to the class. See if the class can think of additional adverbs to add to each diagram.

HOMEWORK

Ask students to observe a person or pet doing something over a three-day period. Have them record the actions by writing a sentence with an adverb modifying a verb. Ask them to highlight the verb and circle the adverb. They should write at least three sentences.

PRACTICE 10: ADVERBS

Underline the adverb in each sentence. In the line after each sentence, write whether the adverb tells *when, where, how,* or *how much.* Score five points for each correct answer. Each sentence needs two answers.

1. My parents went to school here. _____

2. I often visit my grandparents. _____

3. The lion roared loudly. _____

4. My dad snores frequently. _____

5. My friend looked at me shyly. _____

6. We went to the ballgame yesterday. _____

7. We sometimes eat Indian food. _____

8. Let's have a picnic tomorrow. _____

9. When Pablo saw the bear, he barely moved. _____

10. I want to go there for dinner. _____

Cumulative Writing Practice: Using Adverbs Wisely, Explain How to Do Something

Ask students to write a one-paragraph story explaining how to do something (for example: play a sport, play a game, make something like food or a craft). They will use three or four adverbs and highlight them. When they complete their essays, ask the students to work with a partner. Have them look over their partner's work to see if the adverbs were really needed in the story.

Ask them to put a check mark next to the adverbs they agree with and a question mark next to the ones they don't think were necessary to improve the essay. Ask volunteers to share opinions about their partner's adverb usage with the class to see if the class agrees with their comments.

UNIT 7

PREPOSITIONS AND PHRASES

Teacher Tips

Start by explaining to your students that prepositions help add description to sentences. Like adjectives and adverbs, they introduce words (a prepositional phrase) to modify nouns and verbs. Instead of having students memorize prepositions, give them the list of commonly used prepositions (see appendix, Unit 7) and have them become familiar with it.

Tell them that a prepositional phrase begins with a preposition and ends with a noun. We call that noun the object of the preposition. It often contains an article (*a, an, the*).

Next, present examples of sentences with adjectival and adverbial prepositional phrases. Show how the phrases act like adjectives and adverbs to describe nouns, pronouns, and verbs in sentences.

Examples:
  Adjective phrase:
1. We baked two batches of sugar cookies. (*of sugar cookies* modifies *batches*, a noun)

  Adverb Phrase:
1. The doves cooed in the barn. (*in the barn* modifies *cooed*, a verb)

Game: Create a Cluster Poem Using Phrases

This game gives practice using prepositional phrases to modify nouns and verbs in sentences.

Pre-Game Activity

1a. Review the information in unit 6 on how to make a cluster diagram. Students will work independently and will draw a circle and write a noun of their choice inside the circle. They will then put arrows around the circle and attach at least six circles to the main circle. They will fill in these circles with prepositional phrases related to the main circle containing the noun. For example, using *lake* as the noun, a student might use these prepositional phrases to modify it: near my house, around the park, or in the mountains.

1b. Ask volunteers to give examples to the class. Ask the class if they can think of other phrases to modify the nouns the students used. Write them on the board and ask the class to copy the three they like best.

2a. Have students repeat the cluster diagram exercise, this time with adverb phrases. Remind students that adverb phrases are not always next to the verb as they are next to the noun in adjective phrases.

2b. Students will write an action verb in the main circle and draw arrows which give rise to other circles. They will attach at least six circles to the main one and fill in the circles with prepositional phrases related to the verb in the main circle.

Example:

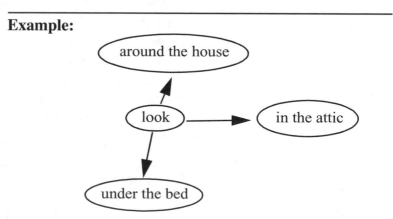

2c. Ask the class to think of more phrases to modify the verbs. Write them on the board as you did with the adjective phrases, and ask students to copy the three phrases they like best.

Lesson Plan

1. Students will write original free-verse poems. Review the explanations of free-verse poetry (see appendix, Unit 1). Also

discuss tone in poetry, pointing out that their poems can be humorous, serious, or thoughtful.

2. Using their cluster diagrams, ask them to write a free-verse poem about a place using at least two adverb phrases and at least three adjective phrases from the cluster diagrams. Have them circle nouns and verbs and underline adjective and adverb phrases. Ask them to write *ADJ* above adjective phrases and *ADV* above adverb phrases.

Sample Cluster Poem
Our Mountain Cabin

We have a cabin *in the mountains*. (adv.)
I love to go there *on weekends*. (adv.)
Mom and I fish *in the lake*. (adv.)
Dad and my brother cook *in the open fire*. (adv.)
Our cabin *on the hill* stands alone, (adj.)
but we have a lot *of company*. (adj.)

Birds fly *around the sky*. (adv.)
Owls hoot *in the trees* (adv.)
at our cabin (adv.) *in the mountains* (adj.)

Note: Point out that the phrase in line #2 modifies *there*, an adverb. Also, ask students what other part of speech *fish* in line #3 can be (it can also be a noun. Here it's used as a verb because it shows action).

| Follow-Up |

1. Ask students to read their poems to the class and have the class name some of the prepositional phrases used in the poems.
2. Ask partners to illustrate their poems with colored markers, crayons, stickers, and glitter. Display the poems in the hall and ask a neighboring class to vote on the best poem.

HOMEWORK

Think of a sentence (example: The cow sleeps). Ask the student to think of adjective phrases (at least three) to describe the subject (examples: *with the brown coat, with the sleepy eyes*). Then ask the student to think of at least three adverb phrases to modify the predicate (examples: *in the meadow, by the river, under the oak tree*). You can call the predicate *verb* at this point since predicate hasn't been introduced yet.

PRACTICE 11: PREPOSITIONAL PHRASES

Underline the prepositional phrases. In the line after each sentence, write *ADJ* for adjective phrases and *ADV* for adverb phrases. Score five points for each correct answer. Each sentence needs two answers.

1. The king and queen live in a castle. _____

2. We swam across the lake. _____

3. I go to the park near my house. _____

4. The dog in the window has shaggy hair. _____

5. We are going to a movie. _____

6. The class will have a pizza party during lunch. _____

7. The tiger with the huge teeth ate steak. _____

8. My kitten hid under the table. _____

9. The baby crawled toward me. _____

10. We bought the iguana with the pretty markings.

Cumulative Writing Practice: Use Phrases To Describe an Animal and Its Actions

Students will write a true or made-up story about an animal they've observed in a zoo, park, or at home. They will use at least three prepositional phrases in the story. Have them underline the phrases, writing *ADJ* above adjective phrases and *ADV* above adverb phrases.

When students complete their first drafts, have them meet with their partners to discuss the phrases they used. They can use these questions as guidelines: Did the phrases begin with a preposition and end with a noun?; Did the partner correctly identify the phrases as adjective or adverb?.

UNIT

8

CONJUNCTIONS

Conjunctions help join words or groups of words in sentences, help create compound sentences, and also work as transitions. For the primary grades, we'll focus on coordinating conjunctions. Teach students the most commonly used conjunctions, *and, but,* and *or,* and show how they work to join words in a sentence.

Game: Join Words with Conjunctions

This game gives practice in joining words and groups of words with conjunctions. It also shows how to write compound subjects and predicates.

Pre-Game Activity

1. Write the conjunctions *and, or,* and *but* on the board. Tell students that *but* is also a conjunction and that we will learn more about it later. Ask students to use each of these conjunctions to connect two nouns, pronouns, or verbs.

   Examples: the teacher *and* the student; he *and* she; today *or* tomorrow, run *or* jump

2. Have students work in groups. On a piece of paper they will make two columns for the conjunctions *and* and *or.* In each column they will write three pairs of nouns and/or pronouns and three pairs of verbs.

61

Examples: nouns: cake *and* ice cream, boys *and* girls; **pronouns**: you *or* I; **verbs**: hop *or* skip, shower *and* dress, smile *and* laugh.

Lesson Plan

1. Students will meet with a partner. Ask each student to write a partial sentence, leaving spaces for pairs of nouns and verbs (compound subjects and verbs) and to write a conjunction between the nouns, pronouns, or verbs.
2. A partner will fill in the blank spaces with nouns and verbs to be joined by the conjunction. For example, for nouns joined by a conjunction, a student might write: _____and_____ are my favorite sports; and the partner might fill in *Football* and *baseball*. For verbs, a student might write: We _____and_____ at the party. The partner might fill in the blanks with *ate* and *played*.
3. Students will exchange papers and check one another's answers.
4. Volunteers will write sentences on the board. Ask the class to identify the conjunctions and to tell whether they join nouns or verbs.

Follow-Up

1. The class will brainstorm different categories of nouns and verbs joined by the conjunctions *and* or *or*. Draw a chart on the board with the following categories and fill it in as they give answers. Nouns: favorite movies, favorite foods, favorite animals, favorite places. Verbs: things I like to do, things I don't like to do, things I do on the weekends.
2. Ask partners to make up their own categories or to use the ones you've given them. They will write three noun or pronoun pairs and two verb pairs.

HOMEWORK

The homework helper writes a pair of nouns for favorite things in four different categories (for example, books, songs, restaurants, stores). The student does the same and they exchange opinions, telling why they chose the things they did.

PRACTICE 12: CONJUNCTIONS

Underline the pairs of words joined by conjunctions. Circle the conjunction. In the space at the end of the sentence, write whether the words joined are **N** (nouns), **P** (pronouns), or **V** (verbs). Score five points for each correct answer. Each sentence needs two answers, one for the pair of words and one for the type of words that the conjunctions join.

1. The zebra and the giraffe smiled for my picture. _____

2. You and I will build a sand castle. _____

3. The baby kicked and splashed in the tub. _____

4. Sarah skipped and hopped. _____

5. Steve and Drew rode their bikes to the store. _____

6. She and I went to the amusement park. _____

7. We dribbled and shot baskets in gym. _____

8. Pizza and tacos are my favorite foods. _____

9. The cow eats and sleeps all day. _____

10. Miguel and María taught me Spanish. _____

<table>
<tr>
<td>

Cumulative
Writing Practice:
Use
Conjunctions to
Connect Words
in a Happy
Memory Story

</td>
<td>

Ask students to write a story about a happy family memory. Have them include at least two nouns, pronouns, or verbs joined by *and* or *or*. Have them highlight these pairs of words and circle the conjunctions. Tell them to underline prepositional phrases and write **ADJ** (adjective) or **ADV** (adverb) above them.

After students complete their first drafts, have them exchange papers with a partner to see whether they joined two nouns, pronouns, or verbs with conjunctions.

</td>
</tr>
</table>

UNIT 9

SIMPLE SENTENCES

A simple sentence contains a complete thought. Learning the components of the simple sentence is the basis for understanding the other sentence types: compound, complex, and compound complex. It is also the best way to ensure that students avoid the major sentence errors, sentence fragments and run-on sentences. If students know that all sentences must contain at least a subject and a verb, they'll be less likely to make these major mistakes in writing.

Explain that when verbs are used in a sentence, they're called predicates. Nouns in a sentence are called subjects or objects. Some sentences may have more than one subject or predicate. We call these compound subjects and compound predicates.

In the previous unit we discussed using the conjunctions *and* and *or* to link nouns, pronouns, and verbs. Now that students know how to use conjunctions to link words, they can learn how to use them in sentences to create compound subjects and predicates.

Your students have already learned many parts of speech. Now they will learn how these parts of speech work to make a sentence.

All sentences must have action. Some sentences contain hidden ("you understood") subjects. These command sentences, like "Leave." and "Eat.", don't have a subject you can see, but they're still sentences. On the other hand, a group of words like *because he woke up late,* is not a sentence because it can't stand alone.

67

Reading or saying the sentence or non-sentence aloud helps develop the students' sense of how to differentiate between a sentence and a sentence fragment. Similarly, when a sentence doesn't stop when it should, reading or saying the sentence can show how a run-on sentence lacks meaning. Teach students to make sense of sentences by helping them develop an ear for how a grammatical sentence sounds.

Game: Stage a Simple Sentence Play

This game teaches students how to identify and write a simple sentence.

Pre-Game Activity

1. Write some simple sentences on the board.

> **Examples:** Shaun threw the ball.
> Jen smiled.
> Move.
> Mom and I went to the play.
> Tyrone clapped and hollered at the game.

Ask how many complete thoughts are in each sentence. Each of these sentences has only one complete thought, and is, therefore, a simple sentence. As you can see, simple sentences can be long or short. Point out that a simple sentence must have a subject and a predicate. It sometimes has an object and other words like adjectives, adverbs, and phrases, but it must always have a subject and predicate to be a sentence. Sometimes sentences have more than one subject or predicate. We call these compound subjects and predicates.

A subject is a noun or pronoun telling what the sentence is about. To find the subject, ask *who* or *what* in front of the predicate or action word. To find the subject in the first sentence, we ask *who threw* and get the answer *Shaun*. The predicate in this sentence is *threw* and the subject is *Shaun*.

Not all sentences have objects, but the first example does. To find the object of the sentence, we reverse what we did to find the subject. We ask *whom* or *what* after the verb. If we ask *threw what*, we get the answer *ball*. *Ball* is the direct object of the sentence.

Sometimes sentences may also have indirect objects. Students have already learned object of the preposition. Indirect objects answer the question *to* or *for whom or what* after the verb.

If we changed the first sentence to "Shaun threw her the ball," *her* is the indirect object. When we asked the question *threw to whom,* we get the answer *her.* (At this stage, use your judgment about whether to teach indirect objects or to confine your discussion of simple sentences to subject, predicate, and direct object.)

The second sentence example has only a subject and predicate, *Jen* and *smiled*. The third has a predicate, *move,* and the subject is "you understood." Although this sentence has a subject, it is not stated.

Students already know how to identify pairs of words (nouns, pronouns, and verbs) joined by conjunctions. To make the leap from words in a sentence to parts of a sentence, all they'll have to do is rename the words. Tell them that they will now call nouns and pronouns joined by conjunctions compound subjects. (Of course, they can also be compound objects of the preposition or compound objects, but this is not in the scope of this book.) Similarly, they will call verbs joined by conjunctions compound predicates.

The fourth example has a compound subject, *Mom and I,* and a prepositional phrase, *to the play,* but it is still a simple sentence. The fifth sentence contains a compound predicate, *clapped and hollered,* and a prepositional phrase, *at the game,* and is also a simple sentence.

2. Ask students to meet in groups and write six examples of simple sentences. They will write at least one command sentence with "you understood" as the subject and at least three examples with objects. They should write at least two with a prepositional phrase. Do not have them label sentence parts.

3. Have the groups exchange papers with another group. Ask them to look at the other group's sentences and label the sentence parts: **S**, subject, **P**, predicate, **O**, object, and **PRP**, prepositional phrase. If you decide to teach the indirect object, have them indicate whether the object is a **DO**, direct object, or an **IO**, indirect object. If not, simply have them write **O**. Have them identify command sentence subjects as **U**, for "you understood", in front of the verb.

4. After students finish the exercise, look at sample sentences on the overhead to validate answers and see if they have any questions.

Lesson Plan

1. Ask groups to write a short skit (1–1 ½ handwritten pages) to perform in front of the class, using all simple sentences. Have them write on one side of the paper and number the pages. The skit can be humorous or serious. The only requirement is that every sentence must have a subject and a predicate. It may or may not have an object or an object of the preposition. It may have a compound subject or a compound predicate, but every sentence must have only one complete thought.

2. After the groups complete their skits, ask them to exchange them with another group to check that the sentences are all simple and are labeled correctly. If they have questions, offer help.
3. Make copies of each one or two page play for everyone in the group. Distribute the copies and have students rehearse in their groups.
4. Students present their skits to the class. After each skit, ask the group to write one of their simple sentences on the board. See if the class can name the subject, predicate, objects, and phrases, and tell why it's a simple sentence.

Follow-Up

1. Invite another class to view the skits. First have students define the parts of a simple sentence and explain that they used all simple sentences in the skits.
2. Ask the visiting class to vote on the best skit and to explain their choice. Have your class make up the standards for voting ahead of time. (The criteria can include interesting plot, lively characters, speaking with expression, and proper grammar.)

HOMEWORK

The homework helper reads a short picture book and asks the student to pick out three simple sentences and to explain why they're simple sentences (one complete thought with a stated or understood subject and a predicate). Subjects and predicates may be compound.

PRACTICE 13: THE SIMPLE SENTENCE

Mark the parts of these simple sentences with the right abbreviations: **S**, subject; **P**, predicate; **O**, object. Write **CS** for compound subject and **CP** for compound predicate. For command sentences, write **U** (understood) at the end of the line. Some sentences might contain a direct and an indirect object. Label them both as **O**. Write the abbreviations above the words in the sentences. If you find an object of the preposition, label it **OP**. You must label the subject, predicate, and object in each sentence to get full credit. Score ten points for each correct sentence.

1. The vet gave my pony a shot.

2. Dad and Mom bought an ice cream cake for my party.

3. Smile.

4. A seagull flew across the sky.

5. The plane roared into the clouds.

6. Our teacher took us to the book fair.

7. We drank ice cream sodas at the diner.

8. I jumped and cheered for our team.

9. Look and listen.

10. My teacher gave us a party.

Cumulative Writing Practice: Write a Paragraph to Persuade Using Simple Sentences

Students will write a persuasive paragraph giving an opinion about something they're concerned about. First, brainstorm ideas with the class. (Examples: We should/shouldn't get homework on weekends.; We should/ shouldn't get paid for chores.) Ask students to suggest a list of topics and write them on the board. Tell them to use at least two simple sentences in their paragraphs and to label the subjects, predicates, objects, and prepositional phrases, using the abbreviations they used in the practice.

Have volunteers read their paragraphs to the class. Ask the class why they thought the essays were convincing, and have them make suggestions to improve the essays. Have each volunteer write one simple sentence on the board. Ask the class to tell why it's a simple sentence.

UNIT 10 COMPOUND SENTENCES

Now that students understand how conjunctions join words in a sentence to create compound subjects and predicates, you can tell them that conjunctions can help them write a new type of sentence, the compound sentence. Unlike simple sentences, compound sentences contain two or more complete thoughts joined by a conjunction. Now students will begin to work more with *but*, another conjunction.

Learning another type of sentence will give students the ability to increase their sentence variety and to add more interest and depth to their writing.

Some students may find it easier to understand the mechanics of a compound sentence if you tell them that there must be a subject and predicate on both sides of the conjunction.

Example: Luz smiled, and her father snapped her picture.

In this sentence *Luz smiled* is the first complete thought. The second complete thought on the other side of the conjunction *and* is *her father snapped her picture*. It's like a simple equation. Both sides must balance out with similar elements.

75

Game: Score Points with Compound Sentences

This game helps students understand the elements of compound sentences and gives practice in writing them.

Pre-Game Activity

1. Show students a simple sentence. Tell them that a simple sentence has one complete thought but that a compound sentence has two or more.

Example of a simple sentence:
   My cat jumped on the table.
Example of a compound sentence using the conjunction *and*:
   My cat jumped on the table, and she ate the fried chicken.

Example of a simple sentence:
   Abe started to sing.
Example of a compound sentence using the conjunction *but*:
   Abe started to sing, but he lost his voice.

Ask the class how the meaning of the conjunction *but* in the second example would differ from the meaning of *and* used in the same sentence. Students may say, "It shows that something different is going to happen."

Pointing out the difference between *and* and *but* will help give your students an understanding of the subtleties of the language. It will show them how they can give the reader clues about what's going to happen next in a sentence or a story.

2. Ask the class to think of twice as many simple sentences as you have groups in your class. Write them on the board and discuss why they are simple sentences.
3. Assign each group two of the sentences. Tell students to turn the simple sentences into compound sentences using *and, but*, or *or*. (Each group must write at least one sentence using *and* and one sentence using *but*.) Ask students to highlight the two complete thoughts in each sentence and to circle the conjunctions.
4. Have the groups present their sentences to the class, explaining why the sentences are compound (two complete thoughts and a conjunction joining the two thoughts).
5. Ask how using *but* is different from using *and*.

| **Lesson Plan** |

1. Plan a compound sentence contest. Divide students evenly into two teams and have them sit opposite each other. Students will respond individually, in the order in which they're seated. Ask the first team to think of a simple sentence. The second team will change it to a compound sentence using *and*. Then ask the second team to think of a simple sentence. The first team will give a compound sentence using *but*.

2. Rotate giving the simple sentence and the compound sentence and the use of *and* and *but* as conjunctions. The team that gets the most points by saying a compound sentence correctly in a given amount of time wins. If a student does not come up with the answer within the time limit, the next team gets a chance to make up a sentence. If a student gives an incorrect answer, the other team gets a chance to give the right answer.

3. Write the compound sentences on the board as the students give them. Have the class choose the most interesting compound sentences, and ask partners to use the sentences as a starting point for writing a "short short" story.

| **Follow-Up** |

1. Ask volunteers to read their stories to the class. Ask them to explain how the compound sentence gave them the idea for their story. (Discussing the creative process gives students an idea of how using a random thought can often spark a story.) Ask them to list other ways they've thought of ideas for writing.

2. Have the class vote on the most interesting story and explain why they chose it.

HOMEWORK

The homework helper writes three simple sentences. The student tells how to change them into compound sentences, identifying the subjects, predicates, and conjunctions of the compound sentences.

PRACTICE 14: SIMPLE AND COMPOUND SENTENCES

In the space before each sentence, write **S** for simple and **C** for compound sentence. Hint: Look for simple sentences with compound subjects or predicates. Score 10 points for each correct answer.

1. _____ Doug painted a picture, and he won a prize.

2. _____ I threw the bone, but the dog didn't catch it.

3. _____ My hamster and gerbil are best friends.

4. _____ We knocked on the door, but no one answered.

5. _____ Lauren sang beautifully and won the contest.

6. _____ Chang planted a tree and watched it grow.

7. _____ Clean your room, or bugs will move in.

8. _____ My friend moved away, but we still visit.

9. _____ Hope loves music and sings in the choir.

10. _____ I built a block castle, but my sister knocked it down.

Cumulative Writing Practice: Write a Character Sketch Using Simple and Compound Sentences

Students will write a character sketch about an important person in their family. They will use strong verbs, descriptive nouns, and will use adjectives, adverbs, and prepositional phrases wisely.

This time they will concentrate on having a good mix of simple and compound sentences in their writing. (Some students may use complex sentences without being aware of it.) Students will use at least three simple and two compound sentences.

They will underline and label the simple, **S,** and compound, **C,** sentences and circle the conjunctions in the compound sentences. After the students consult with their writing partners to see whether they've included both simple and compound sentences, view sample papers on the overhead with the entire class. Have students comment on the effectiveness of paragraph support, the smooth flow of sentences, and the creative use of language.

Here are some questions you might ask: Does the story make sense? Does one idea follow another in a good order? Do the sentences flow smoothly? Do the words sound pleasant to your ear? What did you enjoy most about the story? What changes would you make to improve it?

UNIT 11

SENTENCE PURPOSE

Teacher Tips

Sentences have four different purposes: to tell (declarative), ask (interrogative), command or request (imperative), or show emotion (exclamatory). When you teach the different types of sentences, you can call them telling sentences, asking sentences, commanding sentences, and exclaiming sentences.

Different types of sentences require different punctuation at the end of the sentence. Declarative or telling sentences need a period. Interrogative or asking sentences need a question mark. Imperative or command/request sentences need a period or an exclamation point. Exclamatory sentences always need an exclamation point.

Game: Write Skits Using the Different Types of Sentences

This game explains the different purposes of sentences and shows how to use each. It also emphasizes the proper punctuation of sentences.

Pre-Game Activity

1. Explain the four different types of sentences and write examples on the board without writing what type of sentences they are.

Examples:

Telling Sentence: My friend and I are going to Playland.

81

Asking Sentence: Do you like the roller coaster?
Commanding Sentence: Try the bumper cars.
Exclaiming Sentence: What a wild ride!

2. Ask students to identify each sentence according to purpose and to tell how they would punctuate it. Ask them when they would use an exclamation point with a command/request sentence. (This kind of sentence uses an exclamation point when it expresses strong feelings.)

Lesson Plan

1. Have students work in groups. Ask them to write a four to six sentence mini-skit on a single theme, patterned after the example in the pre-game activity section. Tell them to label the sentences **T**, telling, **A**, asking, **C**, commanding, and **E**, exclaiming. Ask them to write the speakers' names for the skits, which can have from two to four different speakers. They can place the different types of sentences in any order.
2. Have students read their mini-skits to the class. Ask the class to write down the abbreviation for each type of sentence (T, A, C, E) in the order they're read. Ask the group members to verify answers.
3. Ask each group whether they put a period or an exclamation point after their commanding sentence, and have them explain why.

Follow-Up

1. Ask partners to make up a five-sentence practice quiz about different kinds of sentences. Ask them to leave blanks in front of the sentence so that another set of partners can fill them in with the abbreviations: **T,** telling, **A,** asking, **C,** commanding, and **E,** exclaiming. Also, instruct partners to leave out the punctuation so that those taking the quiz can fill it in. Have them write their answer key on a separate sheet.
2. Distribute the practice quizzes to other partners and then return them for marking to the partners who created them. Ask students to score quizzes by writing the number of correct answers at the top. For ease in scoring, have students count correct sentence type but do not count punctuation in the scoring. Discuss punctuation and any answers that cause confusion.

HOMEWORK

The homework helper asks the student to write telling, asking, commanding, and exclaiming sentences related to his or her day.

Examples: (Telling) Today our teacher read us a story about manners.
(Asking) What are we having for dinner?
(Commanding/requesting) Please make French fries instead of rice.
(Exclaiming) Look at that bug on the window!

The helper checks to see if the student wrote one of each type of sentence and also checks punctuation.

PRACTICE 15: SENTENCE PURPOSE

In the space before the sentence, write the type of sentence (**T**, telling, **A**, asking, **C**, commanding or requesting, and **E**, exclaiming). Write the correct punctuation mark at the end of the sentence and circle it. Score five points for giving the right sentence type and five points for using the correct punctuation mark.

1. _____ What a loud roar that bear makes

2. _____ Let's visit the sea lions

3. _____ Would you like some popcorn

4. _____ I saw a peacock spread its wings

5. _____ That elephant might spray you

6. _____ Is the tiger looking at us

7. _____ That ape is playing peek-a-boo

8. _____ Tell me where to meet you

9. _____ Did you see our teacher

10. _____ This was a happy day

> **Cumulative Writing Practice: Write an Opinion Paragraph Using the Different Types of Sentences**

Students will write a paragraph, stating their point of view on a current issue. Ask them how they think they should present their ideas so that people will listen.

Have them brainstorm topics. You may want to offer a couple ideas such as: Year-Round School Is/Is Not a Good Idea, TV Helps/Does Not Help People Learn, or Grounding Is/Is Not a Good Punishment. Ask students to use both simple and compound sentences and to label their sentences **S** for simple, and **C** for compound.

Ask them to write at least one of each kind of sentence and to label them **T** (telling), **A** (asking), **C** (commanding or requesting), and **E** (exclaiming).

Tell them to circle the punctuation of the sentences they labeled. Ask volunteers to read their final drafts to the class. Ask students to vote on the most convincing essay from the ones read and to tell why they felt it was the best essay.

UNIT
12
CAPITAL LETTERS

Teacher Tips

For the most part, learning capitalization involves deciding whether something is general or specific. Common nouns (school, teacher, book) are general and don't need to be capitalized. Proper nouns (Martin Luther King School, Ms. Stein, The Cat in the Hat) are specific and need capitals.

Is it any country or is it America or England? Is it an ordinary egg roll or a Chinese egg roll? Ask students to think back to their study of common and proper nouns and to remember how they always capitalized proper nouns.

Give students examples using capitals in sentences (see rules and examples in the appendix). Students should also know what not to capitalize: namely, directions, seasons, and family titles preceded by a pronoun (my mother), unimportant words in a title like *a, an*, and *the*, and short prepositions and conjunctions (see appendix).

Game: Question and Answer with Capitals

This game teaches students the rules of capitalization and to give them practice using capital letters in their writing.

Pre-Game Activity

1. Tell students that generally common nouns are not capitalized while proper nouns are. Write the following examples on the board.

Person: singer (common noun); Celine Dion (proper noun)
Place: city (common noun); New York City (proper noun)
Thing: team (common noun); Detroit Pistons (proper noun)

2. Ask students to work with a partner and to draw three columns on their paper with the headings *person*, *place*, and *thing*. They will write two common nouns for each category and leave a space under each noun.

3. Partners exchange papers with another set of partners, who will fill in the spaces under the two nouns in each category with proper nouns related to the common nouns. They will give the papers back to the partners who created them to check the answers.

4. Ask partners to write sample common and proper nouns on the board. Have the class check for correct answers and discuss questions.

| Lesson Plan |

1. Give students a hand-out with capitalization rules and examples (see appendix).
2. After going over the rules and examples, ask the class to give their own examples. Write them on the board.
3. Have students meet in groups. Students may refer to their rule and example sheets. Ask groups to write six questions that require a capitalized word as part of the answer. Have them leave three lines after each question.
4. They will exchange their questions with another group, which will answer the questions in complete sentences and circle the words with capital letters. Return papers to the original groups who will check the answers against the rule sheet. Review answers with the class.

Sample Questions and Answers:
Who do you see when you get sick? (I see Dr. Schwartz when I get sick.)
In what city and state does your cousin live? (My cousin lives in Ocean City, New Jersey.)
Name a holiday when you don't have school. (I don't have school on Labor Day.)
What nationality is your family? (My family is African American.)
Which toy store do you like best? (I like The Toy Bin best.)

5. Another time have students repeat the exercise with the rules that apply to words they should not capitalize (seasons, family title with a possessive pronoun, unimportant words in a title).

Have them exchange papers and then discuss answers with the class.

Follow-Up

1. Groups make up a rule booklet for capitalization. They will write one example for each rule, circling the capital letters. They will also write one example for each exception to the rule. They may refer to their rule and example sheets.
2. Tell them to use their imaginations to make their rule booklets unique. They can use drawings, cartoons, glitter, and stickers to decorate their booklets. Ask them to make covers with their own titles.
3. Volunteers share sentences with the class. Post booklets for display.

HOMEWORK

The student reads a story to the homework helper (or the helper reads to a beginning reader). The student finds at least six capital letters in the story and explains why the author used capitals. The helper finds four more instances of capitals and asks the student to tell why the examples need capitals.

PRACTICE 16: CAPITALS

Circle the words that need capitals in each sentence. Each sentence has two examples. Examples may have more than one word. Score five points for each correct answer.

1. We plan to go to new york city to see the play, west side story.

2. I love italian pasta and chinese egg rolls.

3. I saw doctor blanco and aunt Theresa at the football game.

4. My school, hurston elementary, is named for a famous african american writer.

5. We live in the north, and my cousins live in the south.

6. I can't wait for july 4th, but I am a little sad when labor day comes.

7. sofia lives in italy.

8. We visited my cousin in palm beach, florida.

9. I saw rabbi Klein at the hannukah party.

10. The jade garden is my favorite chinese restaurant.

Cumulative Writing Practice: Use Capitals to Make Words Stand Out in a Descriptive Paragraph

Students will write a paragraph about a place they have visited (city, country, tourist attraction, restaurant). They will use at least five words or phrases with capital letters and circle all the capitals, including those at the beginning of sentences.

They will highlight all the action verbs. Have students give their work an original title.

UNIT 13

COMMAS

Teacher Tips

The rules for commas in the early grades require common sense and no complicated rules. Generally, when you read a sentence and need to pause, you use a comma. Commas make sentences clear and help avoid confusion for the reader and the speaker. It's also important not to overuse commas. For example, never use a comma between a subject and a predicate.

Students will learn to use commas

- in a series
- to separate two or more adjectives in front of a noun
- before the conjunctions *and, but,* and *or* in a compound sentence
- after words like *yes* and *no*
- after two or more prepositional phrases that start sentences
- to set off names
- to separate items in dates and addresses
- to open and close friendly letters

Game: Use Commas With Common Sense

This game reviews comma rules and asks students to apply them.

Pre-Game Activity

(Present two or three comma rules each day. Run off the comma rules and examples in the appendix.)

1. Write or have students write examples for each rule (not in order) on the board, without commas filled in.
2. Ask volunteers to read the sentences, fill in the commas, and state the comma rules.

Lesson Plan

1. Ask students to meet in groups. Have them make up a ten-sentence practice quiz with an answer key, using all the comma rules they've learned. Tell them to use strong action verbs in their sentences.
2. Distribute the quizzes to other groups, who will fill in the commas and circle them for easy scoring. Ask students to make the number of commas in the ten questions an even number.
3. Return the quizzes to the groups that composed them and have them check the answers against their answer key. Help with questions and problems.
4. Ask groups to choose the best sentence they wrote using commas. Write the sentences on the board without commas, and ask the class to insert commas where they belong.

Follow-Up

1. Ask partners to write a humorous paragraph using at least three different comma rules. Have them read their paragraphs to the class and explain at least one comma rule they used. Ask them to write their sentence on the board.
2. Ask the class to vote on the best paragraph using the following standards: the paragraph has a beginning, middle, and end; the paragraph uses strong verbs; the paragraph explains one main idea and backs it up with details; and the paragraph flows smoothly from one thought to another.
3. Ask class members to tell why the paragraph stands out.

HOMEWORK

The homework helper reads a short children's story or asks the student to read a book on his or her grade level. Ask the student to explain why the author used commas in at least five instances.

PRACTICE 17: COMMAS

Punctuate the following sentences with commas. Be ready to explain why you used commas in each case. Score ten points for each sentence you punctuated correctly with commas.

1. Binh scored in overtime and our team won the trophy.

2. Yes we are going to the lake this weekend.

3. Len lives at 640 Baker Road Portland Maine.

4. On October 9 2010 my brother will turn sixteen.

5. Over the mountains and through the clouds the birds flew south.

6. Anna wore a green ugly scary costume.

7. We made salad fried chicken and brownies for the picnic.

8. Do you want to play kickball Grace?

9. The cat jumped on my bed but she didn't wake me up.

10. Tessa has a jumpy hungry gigantic rabbit.

From *Quick and Easy Grammar Games to Boost Writing Power*. Copyright © 2006 by Catherine DePino. Westport, CT: Teacher Ideas Press/Libraries Unlimited.

Cumulative Writing Practice: Write a Movie Review Using Commas Correctly

Students will write a review about one of their favorite movies. Why did they like the movie? What did they learn from it? What would they say about it to convince a friend to see it? They will use commas to show at least four rules they've learned.

They will be able to explain how they used each of the comma rules. Remind them to use vivid descriptions with strong verbs and specific nouns. They will use adjectives, adverbs, and phrases wisely. Suggest using a mix of simple and compound sentences. They can try using a short, simple sentence at the beginning or end of the story to create a special effect.

They will meet with their writing partner and review one another's papers to check for comma use.

UNIT
14
MORE
PUNCTUATION

Students have already learned about end marks in unit 11, Sentence Purpose. You may want to review these before teaching more punctuation. In this unit, students will learn how to use apostrophes in contractions and in showing possession. They will also learn how to use quotation marks. Sometimes students have problems telling the difference between contractions and possessive pronouns. Discuss the following examples:

Contraction: It's early.
Possessive Pronoun: Its beak is swollen.
Contraction: Who's the winner?
Possessive Pronoun: Whose idea was that?
Contraction: You're a good friend.
Possessive Pronoun: Your friendship is important to me.
Contraction: They're going to the mountains.
Possessive Pronoun: I love going to their mountain cabin.

Address the importance of proofreading for punctuation. Discuss how using the right punctuation makes good writing look even better. Punctuation is a road map that gives the reader hints about what's coming. It also helps give students a sense of order and organization when they read. Punctuation marks can help show emotion and tell whether the sentence is a statement, a question, or the direct words of a speaker.

Punctuation can also tell how to read aloud what we've written by giving hints about where to pause, what kind of expression to use, and where to stop. It can shorten words into contractions and show ownership. Punctuation helps writers, readers, speakers, and listeners by making ideas clear and manageable.

<table>
<tr><td>

Game: Write Your Own Punctuation Guide

</td></tr>
</table>

<table>
<tr><td>

Pre-Game Activity

</td></tr>
</table>

This game gives practice in explaining the use of selected punctuation marks (commas, apostrophes, and quotation marks) in writing. As with other units containing a lot of information, teach at your own pace.

Apostrophes

1. Discuss the uses of the apostrophe and give examples. Tell students that when they're writing about a serious topic, rather than a lighter topic, it's best to avoid contractions (shortened form of the words using apostrophes). However, when they're telling about something that happened (personal narrative) or describing something, they may use contractions.

We use apostrophes to help shorten two words into one (*do not*, *don't*; *could not*, *couldn't*). Duplicate and distribute the list of contractions in the appendix.

2. Ask partners to write a paragraph on a topic of their choice using six contractions. They may refer to their lists. Have them exchange papers with other partners. Ask them to underline the contractions without looking at their lists and to write the words the contractions represent above the contractions in the paragraph. Go over examples with the entire class.
3. An apostrophe also shows that someone owns something (my friend's video games; her family's camper; Andrew's game). Have students give their own examples of using apostrophes to show ownership, and write them on the board.
4. Ask students to work in their groups. Ask each person in the group to write his or her own sentence describing a favorite possession with an *'s* next to the owner's name. Then have them write another sentence, substituting a pronoun for their names.
5. Have a student from each group read one sentence about each of the student's possessions. Ask the class to write the word that uses an apostrophe and then to substitute a pronoun for that word (*his* or *her*, depending on the reader).

Pre-Game Activity

1. Give students examples of direct and indirect quotations. Use a direct quote to write the exact words someone said. An indirect quote tells what the speaker said, but not in the speaker's exact words. It is what someone else said.

Examples:
> Direct Quote: Mom said, "We are going to the movies this weekend."
> Indirect Quote: Mom said that we were going to the movies this weekend.

---

2. Ask students what types of punctuation and capitalization they would use in direct quotations. (Use a comma after *said* or *asked* and a capital for the first letter of the quote. Place the period or question mark before the quotation mark at the end of the sentence.)

   Ask the class to give examples of direct and indirect quotations.

3. Have partners write five sentences with indirect quotations. Tell them to make up answer keys. Distribute the papers to other partners. Ask them to change the indirect quotations into direct quotations. Return the papers to the original partners, who will check answers and punctuation. Assist with questions.

   A quotation can show up in different positions in a sentence.

Examples:
> Quotation at the beginning of a sentence: "Would you like to go out for ice cream?" Dad asked.
> Quotation at the end of a sentence: Dad asked, "Would you like to go out for ice cream?"

---

4. Ask groups to write a "short short" story (six to eight sentences) using at least one indirect and at least two direct quotations. They will indent each time the speaker changes. Tell them to write **D** (direct) after each direct quotation and **I** (indirect) after each indirect quotation. Ask students to circle all commas and capital letters.

Examples:
> My friend asked if we wanted to go to the mall. (I)
> "I have to clean my room," Kyle said. (D)

"Can we go later?" I asked. (D)
"Maybe we can help Kyle," James said. (D)
"Let's get started, and then we can go," Allan said. (D)
"That's a great idea," said Kyle. (D)

5. Have groups read their stories to the class. Have them show how they punctuated their sentences on the overhead or chalk board. Pay particular attention to end marks, apostrophes, commas, and quotation marks.

Lesson Plan

1. Students meet in groups to write their own punctuation guide. They may refer to the hand-outs, notes, and examples you gave them about commas, apostrophes, and quotation marks.
2. They will define each rule in their own words and will give sentence examples for each. Ask them to give lively examples and to use humor.
3. Have them illustrate their guides with drawings and cartoons and make them colorful.
4. Ask groups to present their guides to the class and to give their most interesting examples. Pass the booklets around, and then post them.

Follow-Up

1. Give the students storybooks at their reading levels. Have them copy five sentences that show the punctuation they've learned.
2. Ask students to present examples from their reading to the class. Have them keep the papers in their writing portfolios.

HOMEWORK

Ask the student to write five direct quotes said by family members during a two-day period. Also ask the student to write one indirect quote.

PRACTICE 18: MORE PUNCTUATION

Punctuate the following sentences correctly. In the space at the end of the sentence, write whether you punctuated for **C**, commas, **A**, apostrophes, or **Q**, quotation marks. (A sentence may need more than one punctuation mark.) Write **I** for indirect quotations. If the sentence doesn't need punctuation, write *none*. Score five points for correct punctuation and five points for naming the type of punctuation.

1. Would you like to go ice skating? asked Ross. _____

2. I ate cotton candy and Dad had a chocolate covered banana. ____

3. My teachers puppy followed her to school. _____

4. Andrew said he wanted to eat Indian food. _____

5. My cat is a slim orange gentle Tabby. _____

6. Luke and Matt rode their mountain bikes along the trail. _____

7. Have a glass of apple cider said Dad. _____

8. We gave the baby books stuffed animals and blocks for her birthday. _____

9. We live in an old warm cozy house. _____

10. In the first quarter of the game Beth scored twelve points. _____

Cumulative Writing Practice: Punctuate a Conversation

Ask students to write a conversation between two people doing something interesting on the weekend. They can base it on a place they have visited or would like to visit with family or friends.

They will circle all punctuation marks (end marks, apostrophes, commas, and quotations). They will exchange papers with writing partners to check punctuation and give ideas to improve the first draft before revising.

UNIT
15

SENTENCE PROBLEMS

RUN-ON SENTENCES AND SENTENCE FRAGMENTS

| Teacher Tips |

Run-on sentences and sentence fragments are two major sentence errors that stand in the way of effective writing. Tell students that run-on sentences don't know when to stop. If you say the sentences, you will usually want to take a breath but can't. There are two types of run-ons. A fused sentence has no punctuation between the two sentences, while a comma splice has a comma between the complete thoughts. Correct run-on sentences by writing two different sentences or by writing a compound sentence.

Examples:

Fused Sentence: Bridget drew pictures on the pavement she used purple chalk.

Corrected Sentence: Bridget drew pictures on the pavement. She used purple chalk. (Write two different sentences.)

Corrected Sentence: Bridget drew pictures on the pavement, and she used purple chalk. (Write a compound sentence.)

Comma Splice: Malik played the piano at the talent show, everyone stood up and clapped.

Corrected Sentence: Malik played the piano at the talent show. Everyone stood up and clapped. (Write two different sentences.)

Corrected Sentence: Malik played the piano at the talent show, and everyone stood up and clapped. (Write a compound sentence.)

A sentence fragment is another major writing error. A fragment is a piece of a sentence that doesn't make sense because it is not a complete thought. If you read it aloud, you'll know you have to add something to make it a complete sentence. Fragments appear in many different forms.

Some fragments don't have a subject.

Example: Went to the park.

Some fragments don't have a predicate.

Example: Shrimp, my dad's favorite seafood.

It's easy to avoid these and other types of fragments if students remember that every sentence must have a subject and a predicate. They should also check that every sentence is a complete thought and can make sense by itself.

Other fragments begin with subordinate clauses.

Example: Because the house was dark.

You don't have to explain subordinate clauses, but you can give some examples of fragments beginning with words like *although*, *since*, *when*, etc.—subordinating conjunctions that introduce subordinate clauses.

Another type of fragment begins with a participial phrase.

Example: Diving in the lake.

Again, you don't have to explain the term. Just give examples of fragments beginning with words with participial endings—words that end in *ing*, *d*, *ed*, *en*, *ing*, *n*, or *t*.

More Examples: Participial Phrase Fragments
1. Jumping rope.
2. Bored with the TV show.
3. Interested in the play.
4. Smiling for the camera.
6. Broken by the baby.
7. Swept out to the ocean.

Naming the types of run-on sentence and fragment errors is not important; getting a sense of how to spot a non-sentence is. Listening to and reading run-ons and sentence fragments will help students differentiate between a complete sentence and a flawed sentence.

Often, students will run out of breath when reading a run-on, and they'll laugh when a classmate tries to read one. When they hear you reading a fragment, they might say, "I don't get it. It doesn't make sense."

Game: Get a Sense for Good Sentences

In this game, students will learn to identify run-on sentences and sentence fragments and will avoid them in writing.

Pre-Game Activity

1a. Write the following run-on sentences on the board or use the overhead.
Ashley forgot her lines in the play the teacher helped her.
Marcus watched the sunset it was pink, purple, and yellow.
1b. Ask students where the first complete thought ends in each sentence (after *play* in the first, and after *sunset* in the second).
1c. Ask how they would correct each sentence. In the first sentence, put a period after *play* and make two sentences, or make a compound sentence using the conjunctions *and* or *but* after *play*. Put a comma before the conjunction. In the second sentence, take out the comma after *sunset*, and use a period.

2a. Write the following sentence fragments on the board or use the overhead.
Amazed by the rainbow.
Surprised by the party.
Since Jamal didn't have school.
Ate the whole flounder.
The huge ship.
Hopping on the sidewalk.
2b. Ask students to correct each sentence fragment by adding words to the partial sentence. Here are some sample corrections.

Amazed by the rainbow, we took a picture of it.
Surprised by the party, Maura started crying.
Since Jamal didn't have school, he slept late.
My Siamese cat ate the whole flounder.
The huge ship docked in New York.
Hopping on the sidewalk, the frog moved toward me.

Although students have not yet studied commas after participial phrases, some will know instinctively to pause at the end of the phrase. Tell students to think about where they'd pause when reading a sentence to help them decide where to place a comma.

Lesson Plan

1. Have students meet with a partner. Ask them to write three humorous run-on sentences and three humorous sentence fragments. Ask them to correct the sentences on a separate answer sheet.
2. Have students read their most humorous sentences to the class. Ask class members to identify whether the error is a run-on or fragment. Ask partners to write their errors on the board, and have class members turn them into correct sentences by using punctuation or by adding words.

Follow-Up

1. For an in-class assignment, ask students to write three run-on sentences and three sentence fragments and then to rewrite the errors correctly.
2. Divide the class into teams. Have teams alternate, reading one of their examples to the other team. Students volunteer to identify the sentence error and tell how to correct it. Alternate among the volunteers to ensure that everyone has a chance to give an answer. The student who made up the sentence verifies the answer. If the student responding answers correctly, his or her team scores a point. The team with the most points wins.

HOMEWORK

The homework helper finds six sentences from a storybook on the child's reading level, and turns them into three run-ons and three sentence fragments. First the helper reads the sentences to see if the student can identify the error, and then the student corrects the error.

PRACTICE 19: SENTENCE PROBLEMS

In the space at the beginning of the sentence, write whether the sentence is a run-on sentence (**RO**) or a sentence fragment (**SF**). Rewrite the sentence in the lines below the sentence mistake. Change the words around any way you want to make a good sentence. Use correct punctuation. Score five points for naming the error and five for correcting the sentence correctly.

1. _____ The Ferris wheel stopped at the top the seats moved back and forth.

   _____

   _____

2. _____ Asked Ravi to lead the parade.

   _____

   _____

3. _____ A gigantic hippopotamus.

   _____

   _____

4. _____ The animals grunted and crowed all night maybe they were having a party.

   _____

   _____

5. _____ Came out of his cave.

   _____

   _____

6. _____ I like bugs I do not like spiders.

   _____

   _____

7. _____ Lightening flashed we ran for cover.

   _____

   _____

8. _____ Along the trail into the woods.

   _____

   _____

9. _____ The frisky pony.

   _____

   _____

10. _____ Rayna made lemonade she forgot to put in the sugar.

   _____

   _____

Final Cumulative Writing Practice: Using Everything You've Learned, Write a Book Review

Ask students to write an essay about one of their favorite books. They will tell what the book is about without giving away the ending and will explain why they would recommend this book to a friend.

Have them check their writing against every point on the checklist before writing their final drafts. For this assignment they may work alone or with a writing partner. By this stage, they will show more confidence in self-editing.

Tell them that they are now powerful writers who can write with ease and confidence. Pass out certificates of achievement for completing this grammar/writing course.

APPENDIX

WRITING CHECKLIST:

Use this list every time you write to proofread your own and your partner's writing. Check off the points that apply to the lessons you've studied. Make changes before writing your final copy.

_____ Wrote good topic sentences (Did the first sentence make you want to read more? Did the title relate to the story's main message?)

_____ Placed ideas in outline in an order that makes sense

_____ Supported topic sentences with details

_____ Moved smoothly from one sentence to another

_____ Wrote an interesting ending (Did the closing sentence sum up the ideas and not leave the reader hanging?)

_____ Used strong verbs

_____ Used specific nouns

_____ Used adjectives, adverbs, and prepositional phrases, but did not overuse them

_____ Used capitals correctly

_____ Used end marks (periods, question marks, exclamation points) correctly

Check that you used these punctuation marks correctly

_____ Commas

_____ Quotation marks

_____ Apostrophes

Check for these two errors. Correct them with strong sentences.

_____ Run-on sentences

_____ Sentence fragments

UNIT 1: POETRY
(FOLLOW-UP), P. 2

You can use the following children's and adult's poetry as examples of free and rhymed verse. Instead, you may want to choose poems you enjoy that correlate with your students' comprehension levels. You can look on the Internet for complete texts of the poems by typing the poem's title and poet's name into a search engine. You can also ask students to suggest their favorite poems.

Childrens' Poetry: Foster, John. *My First Oxford Book of Poems*. Oxford: Oxford University Press, 2000.
Also, see any humorous collections by Shel Silverstein or Jack Prelutsky.

Adult Poems: (Free-Verse) "Fog" by Carl Sandburg; "I Hear America Singing" by Walt Whitman; "This is Just to Say" by William Carlos Williams (Be ready to explain that an ice box is a refrigerator.)

Adult Poems: (Rhymed) "The Bat" by Theodore Roethke; "Stopping by Woods on A Snowy Evening" by Robert Frost; "I'm Nobody! Who Are You?" by Emily Dickinson

UNIT 1: VERB TENSE
(PRE-GAME ACTIVITY), P. 14

Common Irregular Verbs (This is a partial list.)

Present	Past	Past Participle
begin	began	have begun
break	broke	have broken
bring	brought	have brought
burst	burst	have burst
choose	chose	have chosen
do	did	have done
drink	drank	have drunk
drive	drove	have driven
fall	fell	have fallen
give	gave	have given
go	went	have gone
grow	grew	have grown
run	ran	have run
see	saw	have seen
sell	sold	have sold
speak	spoke	have spoken
swim	swam	have swum
take	took	have taken
teach	taught	have taught
throw	threw	have thrown
write	wrote	have written

UNIT 1: IRREGULAR VERB BLOOPERS
(LESSON PLAN), P. 15

The correct answer is in parentheses.

Past Tense Bloopers

break, breaked (broke)
choose, choosed (chose)
fall, falled (fell)
run, runned (ran)
take, taked (took)
freeze, freezed (froze)
know, knowed (knew)

Past Participle Bloopers

have drove (driven)
have ate (eaten)
have froze (frozen)
have spoke (spoken)
have wrote (written)

UNIT 1: SAMPLE PHRASE OUTLINE
(WRITING PRACTICE), P. 18

Topic: Pets
Title: A One in a Million Cat
Topic Sentence: My pet Blanca is no ordinary cat.

1. Big ball of fluff, blue eyes
2. Acts like a person (cries like a human and lets you know what she wants)
3. Gets into trouble (ate a whole chicken left on counter)
4. Follows me everywhere
5. Ending Sentence: Blanca is the best cat friend anyone could have.

UNIT 2: LINKING VERBS
(PRE-GAME ACTIVITY), P. 22

Use these verbs as linking or action verbs:

Feel

Linking Verb: I feel happy.
Action Verb: Feel the dog's soft fur.

Look

Linking Verb: My teacher always looks happy.
Action Verb: Look at that rainbow!

Smell

Linking Verb: The rotten eggs smell terrible.
Action Verb: I smell the pine trees.

Taste

Linking Verb: The fudge tastes creamy.
Action Verb: Taste the sushi.

UNIT 4: DEMONSTRATE PERSONAL PRONOUNS WITH GESTURES
(PRE-GAME ACTIVITY), P. 38

Ask volunteers to demonstrate personal pronouns using gestures or actions. Students can point to themselves to show *I*; point to another student to show *you*; point to a boy for *he*; point to a girl for *she*. The student can bring a couple of other students up to the front of the room to show *we*, and point to a group of students to indicate *they*.

UNIT 4: DEMONSTRATIVE PRONOUNS
(PRE-GAME ACTIVITY), P. 38

Ask volunteers to explain demonstrative pronouns using props like books or school supplies. They can hold objects or point to those close by, saying *this desk* or *these books*. For objects farther away, they can look in the general direction of them and say, *that class* or *those students*. Remind them that *this* and *these* imply closeness while *that* and *those* imply some distance.

UNIT 7: COMMONLY USED PREPOSITIONS
(TEACHER TIPS), P. 55

about	beyond	over
above	by	past
across	down	through
after	during	throughout
against	except	to
along	for	toward
among	from	under
around	in	underneath
at	inside	until
before	into	up
behind	like	upon
below	near	with
beneath	of	without
beside	off	
besides	on	
between	out	

UNIT 12: CAPITAL LETTERS
(TEACHER TIPS), P. 87

EXAMPLES:

Do Capitalize:

A Person's Name:	Emily
The First Letter of a Sentence:	The decorated boats drifted down the bay.
Names of Places:	Tomás lives in Palo Alto, California.
Sections of the Country:	My grandparents live in the South.
Nationalities:	My favorite Chinese food is shrimp fried rice.
Holidays:	Memorial Day starts the summer season.
Brand Names:	I brush with Sparkly Dent Toothpaste every day.
Schools:	Anna attends Howard High School.
Book Titles:	Charlotte's Web made me cry, but it is my favorite book.
Titles of Respect:	Dr. Melissa Chung, our principal, dresses up as a clown for Spirit Day.
Family Titles:	Aunt Shayna always makes me laugh.

Do Not Capitalize:

Directions:	Turn north on Piccadilly Street.
Seasons:	We had an early spring last year. (Capitalize at the beginning of a sentence.)
Family title with a pronoun before it:	Kelly enjoys playing baseball with her father.
Unimportant words in a title:	The Rime of the Ancient Mariner

UNIT 13: COMMAS
(PRE-GAME ACTIVITY), P. 94

a. Commas separate a list of items.

Example: We bought apple juice, carrots, cereal, and ice cream. Place the comma before the last item in the series. The comma in front of the *and* is optional. Decide whether you want to use it. Do the same thing every time you write.

b. Commas separate two or more adjectives in front of a noun.

Example: I brushed my friend's long, curly, tangled hair.

c. Commas separate the complete thoughts in compound sentences. Put them before the conjunctions *and*, *but*, and *or*.

Example: Mom jogged around the block, and Dad rode his bike.

d. Use commas after introductory words in sentences (after *yes*, *no*, or two or more prepositional phrases that start sentences).

Example: (yes, no): Yes, I cleaned my room and fed the bird.
Example: (after two or more prepositional phrases): At the end of the road, I saw a wild horse running.

e. Commas set off names.

Example: (beginning of sentence): Mirta, please feed your goldfish.
Example: (end of sentence): Do you want a burrito, Matt?

f. Commas separate items in dates and addresses.

Example: (date) The twenty-first century began on January 1, 2000.
Example: (address): Ben lives at 21 Blake Street, Philadelphia, PA 19136.
Note: Do not put a comma between the state and the zip code.
Example: My family and I explored the shops at Fifth Avenue, Naples, Florida 34102.

g. Use commas to start and end a friendly letter.

Example: (to start a friendly letter): Dear Beth,
Example: (to end a friendly letter): Sincerely,

UNIT 14: MORE PUNCTUATION—APOSTROPHES (CONTRACTIONS)

(PRE-GAME ACTIVITY), P. 100

I am	(I'm)
let us	(let's)
she would	(she'd)
they had	(they'd)
we are	(we're)
where is	(where's)
you will	(you'll)
is not	(isn't)
do not	(don't)
does not	(doesn't)
will not	(won't)
has not	(hasn't)
should not	(shouldn't)
were not	(weren't)
can not	(can't)

ANSWER KEY

UNIT 1

Practice 1: Strong Action Verbs

Sample sentences accompany correct answers. Students will offer additional sentences.

1. (c) The hungry dragon ate candy.
2. (a) The polite zebra never burps.
3. (b) The sleepy baby yawns.
4. (c) The friendly teacher always smiles.
5. (a) The sick elephant coughs.
6. (b) The sad clown never chuckles.
7. (a) The reindeer sneezes often.
8. (c) My mom builds bridges.
9. (c) My grandmother drives a bus.
10. (a) My father jogs every day.

Practice 2: The Right Verb

1. tiptoed	4. scampered	7. licked	10. giggled
2. stroked	5. fetched	8. jogged	
3. scurried	6. baked	9. rolled	

Practice 3: Verb Tense

1. b, present (Clue: He plays every night so it's present tense)
2. a, future (Clue: She will chase the gerbil if it escapes).
3. b, past (Clue: We laughed when the cat ate the tuna. Both happened in the past).
4. a, future (Clue: We will build it when it snows in the future).
5. b, past (Walked and said are both in the past tense.)
6. a, future (Clue: They will play tag if it does not rain in the future.)
7. a, past (Clue: Tossed and scored are both in the past tense.)
8. b, future (Clue: Next week tells you to use future tense.)
9. a, present (Clue: Every time tells you to use present tense.)
10. b, past (Clue: Tasted and made are both in the past tense.)

Practice 4: Irregular Verbs

1. b 2. a 3. b 4. a 5. a 6. b 7. b 8. a 9. b 10. b

UNIT 2

Practice 5: Linking Verbs

1. was   2. were   4. are   4. is   5. am   6. A   7. L   8. A   9. A   10. L

UNIT 3

Practice 6: Common Nouns and Proper Nouns

1. C, airplane; P, New York
2. P, Mr. Plunket; C, violin
3. C, mother; P, Kalamazoo
4. P, Mrs. Pringle; C, clown
5. C, popcorn; P, Princeton Mall
6. P, Lincoln; C, money
7. C, apple cake; P, The Cake Factory
8. C, alligator; P, Florida
9. C, seagull; P, Atlantic Ocean
10. C, mouse; P, Mr. Cheese Please

Practice 7: Specific Nouns

1. b   2. a   3. b   4. a   5. b   6. b   7. a   8. b   9. b   10. b

UNIT 4

Practice 8: Pronouns

1. what, that   4. which, us   7. this, he   10. we, them
2. you, it   5. she, it   8. those, its
3. I, my   6. my, its   9. they, our

UNIT 5

Practice 9: Adjectives

(Suggested Answers) Students will offer other ideas.

1. sticky   4. frisky   7. close   10. beautiful
2. gigantic   5. silly   8. colorful
3. warm   6. delicious   9. interesting

UNIT 6

Practice 10: Adverbs

1. here, where
2. often, how much
3. loudly, how
4. frequently, how much
5. shyly, how
6. yesterday, when
7. sometimes, how much
8. tomorrow, when
9. barely, how much
10. there, where

UNIT 7

Practice 11: Prepositional Phrases

1. in a castle, ADV
2. across the lake, ADV
3. near my house, ADJ
4. in the window, ADJ
5. to a movie, ADV

6. during lunch, ADV
7. with the huge teeth, ADJ
8. under the table, ADV
9. toward me, ADV
10. with the pretty markings, ADJ

UNIT 8

Practice 12: Conjunctions

1. The zebra and the giraffe, N
2. you and I, P
3. kicked and splashed, V
4. skipped and hopped, V
5. Steve and Drew, N

6. She and I, P
7. dribbled and shot, V
8. pizza and tacos, N
9. eats and sleeps, V
10. Miguel and María, N

UNIT 9

Practice 13: The Simple Sentence

1. vet, S; gave, P; pony, O; shot, O
2. Dad and Mom, CS; bought, P; ice cream cake, O; party, OP
3. (Subject), U; smile, P
4. seagull, S; flew, P; sky, OP
5. plane, S; roared, P; clouds, OP
6. teacher, S; took, P; us, O; book fair, OP
7. We, S; drank, P; ice cream sodas, O; diner, OP
8. I, S; jumped and cheered, CP; team, OP
9. (Subject), U; Look and listen, CP
10. teacher, S; gave, P; us, O; party, O

UNIT 10

Practice 14: Simple and Compound Sentences

1. C   2. C   3. S   4. C   5. S   6. S   7. C   8. C   9. S   10. C

UNIT 11

Practice 15: Sentence Purpose

1. E, exclamation point
2. C, period
3. A, question mark
4. T, period
5. T or E, period or exclamation point

6. A, question mark
7. T or E, period or exclamation point
8. C, period
9. A, question mark
10. T or E, period or exclamation point

UNIT 12

Practice 16: Capitals

1. New York City, West Side Story
2. Italian, Chinese
3. Doctor Blanco, Aunt Theresa
4. Hurston Elementary, African American
5. North, South

6. July, Labor Day
7. Sofia, Italy
8. Palm Beach, Florida
9. Rabbi, Hanukkah
10. Jade Garden, Chinese

UNIT 13

Practice 17: Commas

1. overtime, (in compound sentences)
2. Yes, (after certain words that begin a sentence)
3. Road, Portland, (address)
4. 9, 2010, (dates)
5. clouds, (after two or more phrases that begin sentences)
6. green, ugly, (to separate two or more adjectives in front of a noun)
7 salad, chicken, (to separate a list of items. Comma after chicken is optional.)
8. kickball, (to set off names)
9. bed, (in compound sentences)
10. jumpy, hungry, (to separate two or more adjectives in front of a noun)

UNIT 14

Practice 18: More Punctuation

1. "Would skating?": Q
2. candy,: C
3. teacher's,: A
4. none,: I
5. slim, orange,: C

6. None
7. "Have cider,": C, Q
8. books, animals, (optional comma after animals): C
9. old, warm,: C
10. game,: C

UNIT 15

Practice 19: Sentence Problems (Suggested Answers)

1. RO: (Two Sentences) The Ferris wheel stopped at the top. The seats moved back and forth. (Compound Sentence) The Ferris wheel stopped at the top, and the seats moved back and forth.
2. SF: The teacher asked Ravi to lead the parade.
3. SF: A gigantic hippopotamus smiled at me.
4. RO: (Two Sentences) The animals in the park grunted and crowed all night. Maybe they were having a party.
   Note: Ask students why it is best to separate this run-on sentence into two sentences. Answer: Correcting it with a conjunction isn't a good idea because the sentence would not make good sense.
5. SF: The hungry bear came out of his cave.
6. RO: (Two Sentences) I like bugs. I do not like spiders.
   (Compound Sentence) I like bugs, but I do not like spiders.
   Note: Ask why it would sound better to use the second example. Answer: In the second example, the conjunction *but* gives a hint that a change in thought is coming.
7. RO: (Two Sentences) Lightening flashed. We ran for cover. (Compound Sentence) Lightening flashed, and we ran for cover.
   Note: Ask students which choice they would prefer. Answer: In this case, two simple sentences will work well because it shows the urgency of the situation. The strong verbs and short sentences create a sense of action. However, either option is acceptable.
8. SF: My scout troop hiked along the trail into the woods.
9. SF: The frisky pony jumped over the fence.
10. RO: (Two Sentences) Rayna made lemonade. She forgot to put in the sugar. (Compound Sentence) Rayna made lemonade, but she forgot to put in the sugar. Note: Ask why, in this case it is better to use *but* rather than *and*. Answer: *But* gives a hint that the thought will change to something different. It gives the reader a clue about what's to come.

INDEX

ABOUT THE AUTHOR

DR. CATHERINE SPINELLI DEPINO is an assistant professor of education and a student teaching supervisor for Temple University. She has written grammar books for elementary and secondary students; two spiritual books for teenagers: *Hi, God It's Me: E-Prayers for Teenage Boys* and *Hi, God It's Me: E-Prayers for Teenage Girls*; and a chapter book, *Blue Cheese Breath and Stinky Feet: How to Deal with Bullies* (2004). For many years she served as an English teacher and department head in the Philadelphia School District. This book comes out of her belief that grammar, if taught holistically, helps produce superior writers.

DATE DUE

ABOUT THE AUTHOR

DR. CATHERINE SPINELLI DEPINO is an assistant professor of education and a student teaching supervisor for Temple University. She has written grammar books for elementary and secondary students; two spiritual books for teenagers: *Hi, God It's Me: E-Prayers for Teenage Boys* and *Hi, God It's Me: E-Prayers for Teenage Girls*; and a chapter book, *Blue Cheese Breath and Stinky Feet: How to Deal with Bullies* (2004). For many years she served as an English teacher and department head in the Philadelphia School District. This book comes out of her belief that grammar, if taught holistically, helps produce superior writers.